DATE DUE

american indian tribal courts

The Costs of Separate Justice

80199

american indian tribal courts

The Costs of Separate Justice

Samuel J. Brakel

Chicago   American Bar Foundation   1978

Samuel J. Brakel is a Research Attorney at the
American Bar Foundation

Publication of this volume by the American Bar
Foundation signifies that the work is regarded as
valuable and responsible. The analyses, conclusions,
and opinions expressed are those of the author and
not those of the American Bar Foundation, its officers
and directors, or other persons or institutions associated
with its work.

Library of Congress Catalog Card Number: 78-67458

ISBN 0-910058-92-X

PRINTED IN U.S.A.

THE AMERICAN BAR FOUNDATION is engaged in research on legal problems and the legal profession. Its mission is to conduct research that will enlarge the understanding and improve the functioning of law and legal institutions. The Foundation's work is supported by the American Bar Association, the American Bar Endowment, The Fellows of the American Bar Foundation, and by outside funds granted for particular research projects.

Acknowledgments

Lucille Alaka for manuscript editing
Holly Colman and Bette Sikes for copyediting
Joanne Watson and Linda Modrowski for typesetting
A. Darryl Beck for production
Jan Madsen for typing the manuscript

contents

american indian tribal courts

The Costs of Separate Justice

INTRODUCTION: SCOPE AND METHOD

Today many American Indian tribes are attempting to deal with the civil and criminal problems on their reservations through their own tribal courts.[1] Few people in this country—including lawyers—are aware of the existence of this separate and semiautonomous Indian court system, and even fewer have any idea of how it operates. It is worthwhile, therefore, to acquaint both the general public and members of the legal profession with the workings of this system.

To study and to report on a topic as broad as "the tribal court system" is a very ambitious task, yet one that deserves to be undertaken for several reasons. (1) Despite the popularity of, and preoccupation with, so many other Indian issues and problems—particularly the dramatic political, legal, and philosophical ones—almost nothing is known or written about the day-to-day affairs of contemporary reservation life, which include the opera-

---

1. "Tribal court" is used here as a general descriptive term. It has sometimes been used as a term of art to distinguish one type of court—historically, politically, and organizationally—from two other types of Indian courts: the "traditional," or "custom," courts, found primarily on the Pueblo reservations in New Mexico, and the "Courts of Indian Offenses," the BIA-created and controlled courts that predate the currently predominant tribal courts (see further textual discussion).

1

tions of the tribal courts.[2] It is important to acquaint the public—whether simply interested citizens or potential decision makers—with these mundane facets of Indian life. (2) Because of

---

2. There is a wealth of literature, including "legal" literature, on Indian matters, but it rarely deals with contemporary issues. Apart from a few short pieces dealing mainly with the theory rather than practices, there is no legal literature on the present-day tribal court system. Instead the bulk of it concerns jurisdictional issues and treaty rights on land or water use. A quick look under the category of "Indians," in the Index to Legal Periodicals, for example, reveals a preponderance of articles dealing with jurisdictional and substantive Indian "claims." In addition, there are studies with an anthropological focus—typically, historical quests to uncover the traditional "law-ways" of selected tribes. See, e.g., Karl N. Llewellyn & E. Adamson Hoebel, The Cheyenne Way: Conflict and Case Law in Primitive Jurisprudence (Norman: University of Oklahoma Press, 1941); Watson Smith & John M. Roberts, Zuni Law: A Field of Values (Papers of the Peabody Museum of American Archaeology and Ethnology, Harvard University, vol. 43, no. 1) (Cambridge, Mass.: Harvard University, Peabody Museum, 1954). Another example is the research presently being done at the University of Alaska (Institute of Social, Economic, and Government Research) by Professors Arthur E. Hippler and Stephen Conn on the law-ways of Alaska Eskimo and Indian groups.

Also common are all-purpose, textbook-like treatments that attempt to deal with the "entire Indian business"—historical, political, and legal; contemporary reservation conditions and institutions are by and large excluded. One of the more valuable publications of this genre is William A. Brophy & Sophie Aberle, eds., The Indian—America's Unfinished Business (Norman: University of Oklahoma Press, 1966). Also, Monroe E. Price, Law and the American Indian: Readings, Notes, and Cases (Contemporary Legal Education Series) (Indianapolis: Bobbs-Merrill Co., 1973); and Theodore W. Taylor, The States and Their Indian Citizens (Washington, D.C.: Bureau of Indian Affairs, 1972). Finally, of course, there is the political, hysterical, or plain "rip-off" literature that trades on popular romantic interest in, or white American guilt and bias toward, the Indian's condition. (One need only look at the covers and flip through the pages in any of the rows of Indian-related publications in popular, and even academic, bookstores.) Stan Steiner's The New Indians (New York: Harper & Row, 1968) is one of the better-known books of the political-polemical type. Its value lies in its capturing rather well the personalities and world views of the new Indian leaders. Its flaw lies in its totally uncritical presentation of what is essentially an extreme and xenophobic outlook and in the implication that it represents the views of the average Indian. In fact, much of what is reported in Steiner is no more than the rhetoric—albeit increasingly popular rhetoric—of an angry and vocal fringe group of self-appointed spokesmen and leaders. For every "new Indian" who goes about juxtaposing a caricature of white values (evil) against Indian values (good), there are 10 "old Indians" who are aware of the unreality of this juxtaposition and of the diversity within so-called white and Indian values and of the commonality between them. For every Indian leader who points his finger at the white system, there are 10 Indian nonleaders who recognize the arrogance of and inconsistencies in this exercise. For every one of Steiner's "Red Muslims" shouting "Red Power," there are 10 "nondenominational" Indians who are indifferent to such sloganizing and 10 more who are convinced that red power only means that Indian authorities rather than white ones will exploit them. Practically the only works that deal specifically with the contemporary tribal court system are the reports of the Senate Hearings on the Constitutional Rights of the American Indian (Hearings Before the Subcomm. on Constitutional Rights of the Senate Comm. on the Judiciary, 87th Cong., 1st Sess., 89th

the general ignorance about the tribal court system, one is obliged to cover the whole of it if one discusses it at all. It makes little sense to focus on some select part of the operations—as research projects typically do—when there is no appreciation of the whole; no part can be understood in isolation. On the other hand, it has not been possible to treat the whole system in great depth, but rather only lightly and impressionistically. A good portion of this report, as a result, reads like and essentially is field notes and observations.

The *method* of study, in turn, was dictated by its scope. It was influenced, in addition, by such realities as the lack of dependable and complete records on tribal court operations. (Similar problems would affect a study of non-Indian lower courts—sometimes even the higher courts.) In any case, these factors explain why a combination of observation and interviews was used as the main *way* of collecting information. The main *subjects* of observation were the proceedings of the courts and the conduct of the participants—judges, litigants, and any representatives of the latter. To complement the observations, these participants in the court process were also interviewed. Naturally, the actions and views of supporting personnel—for example, law enforcement, probation, welfare, and Bureau of Indian Affairs (BIA) officials—also deserved and received attention. For comparative purposes, observations were made and interviews were conducted in county and district courts in areas immediately adjacent to the reservations.[3] Also, visits were made

---

Cong., 1st Sess. (1961-65)). The limitations in terms of coherence and depth are inherent in the format of these proceedings, of course. Moreover, as their title indicates, the hearings were focused primarily on the application or applicability of constitutional rights on the reservations; this singularity of purpose eventually led to the passage of the Indian Bill of Rights of 1968 (25 U.S.C. secs. 1302-3 (1975 Supp.), originally Pub. L. No. 90-284, tit. II, 82 Stat. 77 (1968)), which in turn has dictated and narrowed the focus of much of the writing on Indian law since that date. (See the *Index to Legal Periodicals* and the focus indicated by the titles and contents of the following recent articles: Note, The Indian Bill of Rights and the Constitutional Status of Tribal Governments, 82 Harv. L. Rev. 1343 (1969); James R. Kerr, Constitutional Rights, Tribal Justice, and the American Indian, 18 J. Pub. L. 311 (1969); Note, Indian Tribal Courts and Procedural Due Process: A Different Standard? 49 Ind. L.J. 721 (1974).)

3. The term "regular courts" is used interchangeably throughout this report with "Anglo-American courts," "white courts," or "non-Indian courts." All are awkward, but they are necessary to distinguish them from the "Indian" or "tribal" courts. No negative connotation or regional flavor is intended.

to several reservations under state and county jurisdiction to get a feel for the efficacy of that arrangement. Because they were informal—no questionnaires were used—the interviews varied greatly in length and scope; some lasted only 10-15 minutes, while others took one or several sessions of from 3-4 hours to a full day. Most informants were either directly or indirectly connected with the courts or law enforcement agencies. Occasionally, however, the views of the "man in the street" or official or unofficial spokesmen—both on and off the reservation—were sought. All observing and interviewing were done by the author of this report.

To help interpret the first-hand information, the legal and anthropological literature on the American Indian as well as writings on a number of other ethnic, tribal, and national groups were consulted. The footnotes and explicit comparative references in the text will indicate the range of this background reading.

Five reservations with operating tribal courts were visited: the Standing Rock Sioux Reservation (North and South Dakota); the Devils Lake Sioux (Fort Totten) Reservation (North Dakota); the Uintah and Ouray Ute Reservation (Utah); the Blackfeet Reservation (Montana); and the Navajo Nation (Arizona and New Mexico; another small portion of the Navajo Reservation in Utah was not visited). In addition, seven tribes without tribal courts which were under regular state jurisdiction were included in the study: the White Earth Reservation and the Leech Lake Reservation (Minnesota; Leech Lake has a tribal "conservation" court that deals with hunting and fishing violations committed by Indians, but otherwise the residents are subject to the state and county court system); the Eastern Cherokee Reservation (North Carolina); and the Pawnee, Osage, Western Cherokee, and Creek tribes (Oklahoma). Usually a week was spent on each reservation; however, a week and a half was spent on the Navajo Reservation; the two Minnesota reservations were done together in one week; and the four Oklahoma tribes were covered in one week. In Minnesota, a study of the Red Lake Reservation, along with the recently "retrocessed"[4] Nett

---

4. For years, culminating in the early 1950s, the dominant policies were "assimila-tion" and "termination" of reservation status; over the past decade, the trend has

Lake Reservation, the only reservations in the state with tribal courts, had to be abandoned when the chairman of the tribe refused to grant permission. During the exploratory stages of the study, when limiting the fieldwork to one state was considered, the Turtle Mountain Chippewa Reservation and the Fort Berthold Reservation (North Dakota) were each visited for half a day. But no follow-up was made when it became clear that studying tribes of a greater geographical diversity was desirable. To take a quick look at the state and county court systems in areas surrounding the reservations meant spending a day or two in such places as McLaughlin and Lemmon, South Dakota; Devils Lake, North Dakota; Cut Bank, Montana; Gallup and Cortez, New Mexico; and Roosevelt, Utah.

Something perhaps best described as background fieldwork took place in Salt Lake City and Washington, D.C., where contacts were made and interviews were held with representatives of some of the many "Indian" organizations, groups, and departments (including Interior). In Denver, a training conference for Indian court judges was attended.

TRIBAL COURTS:
HISTORY, JURISDICTION, AND CURRENT STATUS

Tribal courts exist today on some 60 to 120 Indian reservations, depending on the definitions of "courts" and "reservations."[5] Most of these reservations, and the major ones in terms of area and population, are located in the northern plains and Rocky Mountain states, particularly Arizona, New Mexico, Montana, and the Dakotas. For a variety of historical reasons—

---

been "restoration" or "retrocession" of tribal/reservation status under federal trust (see textual discussion further on).

5. The "estimate" (only an estimate is possible, given the variance in the figures available) of 60 tribal courts comes from sources like Kerr, *supra* note 2; and Hearings Before the Subcomm. on Constitutional Rights, *supra* note 2, at 252-53 (app. J). A count of 120-odd courts was reported in a recent article by Robert L. Simson, who cited the BIA as source (Wall Street J., Dec. 28, 1976, at 1, col. 4). The difficulty is that there has never been a clear and fixed definition of "reservation" and "tribal court." Today the estimate of 60 is conservative; it is limited to the more clearly established reservations and courts and fails to include a number of recently retrocessed reservations. The estimate of 120, on the other hand, must include many smaller and less-established Indian landholdings and courts of more limited jurisdiction (such as tribal "conservation" courts, which handle only violations of fishing and hunting regulations).

some relatively recent[6] —having to do with degree of acculturation or dispersal or simply with the smallness of the Indian
tribes and bands in other parts of the country, the Indian people
in these parts, even if still living on "reservations" or otherwise
designated Indian landholdings, are—with a few exceptions—
subject to state court jurisdiction.

The theory behind the self-government power of the American Indian tribes, including the power to regulate their affairs
through an adjudicative system, is that this power derives from
an original sovereignty, which, though limited through wars,
treaties, constitutional language, and congressional action, has
never been fully extinguished.[7] Jurisdictional conflicts concerning this theory have occurred, and continue to exist, on two
levels: federal versus tribal, and state versus tribal.

In the struggle between state and tribal power, the federal
government—most frequently the federal courts, including the
U.S. Supreme Court—has been cast in the role of protector of
the vestiges of tribal sovereignty. Chief Justice Marshall, in two
cases involving the Cherokee tribe decided in the early 1830s,
became one of the earliest and primary architects of tribal
sovereignty: in *Cherokee Nation v. Georgia*,[8] the Court designated the Indian tribes "domestic dependent nations," and in
Worcester v. Georgia,[9] it held that the "laws of Georgia can
have no force [in the Cherokee Nation]," thus first establishing
the principle of federal protection of what was left of tribal
autonomy.

The federal government, however, has not always followed

---

6. The more recent history bearing on the jurisdictional issue involves the transient
congressional commitment to the policy of "termination" (of reservation status)
during the 1950s and early 1960s, which began with the sweeping legislation of Pub.
L. No. 280, ch. 505, 67 Stat. 588 (codified as 18 U.S.C. sec. 1162 (1974 Supp.)) and
resulted in the specific termination of two relatively major tribes—the Wisconsin
Menominees (since reestablished as a tribe) and the Oregon Klamaths—as well as some
60 other small groups or bands of Indians and mixed-bloods; in the late 1960s this
commitment was ultimately reversed through a series of legislative actions and executive pronouncements. See note 13 and accompanying text *infra*.
7. See Richard P. Fahey, The Vestiges of Sovereignty 3 (1974) (unpublished
manuscript available through the Navajo court), citing Felix S. Cohen, ed., Handbook
of Federal Indian Law 122 (1942).
8. 9 U.S. (5 Pet.) 178 (1831).
9. 10 U.S. (6 Pet.) 214 (1832).

this principle with consistency and clarity. In fact, on the issue of tribal sovereignty, vacillation may be the most salient characteristic of federal policy. The Dawes Act (or General Allotment Act) of 1887,[10] which was aimed primarily at breaking up the reservation system; the Indian Reorganization Act of 1934,[11] which reversed that policy; the announcement of the "Termination Policy" in 1953,[12] and the repudiation of that policy in the late 1960s[13] are general examples. On the specific issue of court jurisdiction, the Major Crimes Act of 1885[14] and the Indian Civil Rights Act of 1968[15] illustrate the federal policy of restricting the juridical powers of the tribe in the face of the broad language of, and philosophy behind, the Marshall cases and similar pronouncements.

The Major Crimes Act was the congressional response to the problem of jurisdictional vacuum indicated in *Ex Parte Crow Dog*,[16] a case in which the U.S. Supreme Court had reversed the federal district court conviction of an Indian charged with killing a fellow tribesman, on grounds that the laws of the United States did not apply to acts of Indians in Indian country. The act specified 7 major crimes that would fall within the jurisdiction of the federal courts if committed by Indians in Indian country. The list has since been extended to cover 13 crimes: murder; manslaughter; rape, carnal knowledge of any female, not his wife, who has not attained the age of 16 years; assault with intent to commit rape; incest; assault with intent to kill; assault with a dangerous weapon; assault resulting in serious bodily injury; arson; burglary; robbery and larceny.[17] The federal statute uses the word "exclusive" in listing the crimes that come

---

10. Ch. 9, 25 U.S.C. (1970); originally ch. 119, 24 Stat. 388 (Feb. 8, 1887).
11. 25 U.S.C. sec. 461 (1970); originally ch. 576, 48 Stat. 984 (1934).
12. *Supra* note 6.
13. See address to the Congress of the United States by President Nixon, July 8, 1970, cited in Deborah Shames, ed., Freedom with Reservation, The Menominee Struggle to Save Their Land and People 16 (Madison, Wis.: National Committee to Save the Menominee People and Forests, 1972).
14. 18 U.S.C. sec. 1153 (1970); originally ch. 341, sec. 9, 23 Stat. 385 (1885).
15. 25 U.S.C. secs. 1302-03 (1970); originally Pub. L. No. 90-284, tit. II, 82 Stat. 77 (1968).
16. *Ex parte* Crow Dog, 109 U.S. 556 (1883).
17. 18 U.S.C. sec. 1153 (1970).

within federal jurisdiction; arguments persist and are increasing that the tribes should retain concurrent power to handle these cases, although at present no tribe asserts this in practice.[18] Operationally, federal jurisdiction over major crimes means an FBI presence on the reservations and sporadic litigation in federal courts usually far removed from the scene of the crime and the residences of the accused, witnesses, and victims.

The 1968 Indian Civil Rights Act is the culmination of hearings conducted during the 1960s before the Senate Committee on the Judiciary, Subcommittee on Constitutional Rights. These hearings, which were held across the country and on location at (or near) Indian reservations as well as in Washington, focused on the constitutional rights of the American Indian and elicited considerable testimony from Indian witnesses to the effect that these rights were frequently denied by tribal courts and governments. The solution was seen to rest in the enactment of a bill of rights for Indians, modeled on the Bill of Rights of the United States Constitution. Two provisions of the act make concrete the limits to be placed upon and the principles to be followed by the tribes: (1) no tribe shall imprison a convicted offender in excess of six months or exact a fine of over $500, and (2) habeas corpus is available to any Indian who wants to test (in the federal courts) the legality of his detention by a tribe.

Together, then, the Major Crimes Act and the Indian Civil Rights Act make drastic inroads on the juridical sovereignty of the tribes. Other, often self-imposed, limitations exist as well. In theory, the tribal courts are left with jurisdiction over all civil and criminal matters that occur within reservation boundaries with the exception of the 13 federal crimes as long as "due process" is observed in criminal cases. The fact is, however, that many tribal courts have either ceded or never assumed jurisdiction over one or more of the following areas: probate, juvenile problems, domestic relations, housing issues, and the like—matters in which special laws, expertise, or facilities were perceived to be needed but lacking. In general, moreover, the

18. See Indian L. Rep., Mar. 1974, at 53-58.

tribal courts—with a few rare exceptions—have refused to take jurisdiction over non-Indians who engage in illegal transactions or commit offenses on reservation property, despite the fact that a good argument can be made for their having this power[19] and that non-Indians clearly can, and sometimes do, sue Indians in the tribal courts.

Perhaps the most significant fact about the origin and development of the tribal courts is that they are white American creations, and quite recent ones at that.

Historically, law, order, and justice in Indian societies were dispensed in widely varying ways, matching the wide variety in cultures and life-styles among the tribes. Much was left to private means of enforcement—appropriate action in many conflict situations being the responsibility of the family or clan. If resort to more public means was had, it might be to political (tribal) councils, soldier or hunter societies, secular or religious leaders, generally respected and/or elder individuals, or combinations of these. But there were no "courts" and "judges" in the sense of the "independent" and "exclusively adjudicative" institutions and personnel that Anglo-American ideals have them to be. Nor, of course, were there public jails, prosecutors and police, written codes and cases, civil-criminal distinctions, and other standard attributes of the Anglo-American justice system. Actions on the order of banishment, public ridicule, and restitution played large roles in traditional Indian dispute resolution and behavior control. Retaliatory (private) and retributive (public) death and mutilation were also known forms of "punishment."[20]

The traditional law-ways of the vast majority of the Indian

---

19. E.g., see Indian L. Rep., Feb. 1974, at 51. Also, Fahey, *supra* note 7, at 20-21. But in the past few years several tribes have begun to think about, and a few have in fact begun, asserting such authority. This trend appears to have been a short-lived one: just a few months ago (March 1978), the U.S. Supreme Court in Oliphant v. Suquamish Indian Tribe, 55 L. Ed. 2d 209, 48 U.S.L.W. 4210, 435 U.S. ____ (1978), held definitively that the tribes do *not* have jurisdiction over non-Indians.

20. See, e.g., Llewellyn & Hoebel, *supra* note 2; E. Adamson Hoebel, The Law of Primitive Man: A Study in Comparative Legal Dynamics (New York: Atheneum, 1968); Laura Nader, ed., Law in Culture and Society (Chicago: Aldine Publishing Co., 1969), particularly the contribution by E. Adamson Hoebel, Keresan Pueblo Law, at 92-116; and Smith & Roberts, *supra* note 2.

tribes, however, were lost—completely or nearly so—during the process of physical displacement and decimation which constitutes their history and by the subsequent generations of reservation life and exposure to white society. In the late 1800s the Bureau of Indian Affairs (BIA) created the Courts of Indian Offenses.[21] The purpose of these courts, according to their BIA creators, was to promote acculturation and control on the reservations, which were faring badly in both respects. The judges of these courts were Indians appointed by and responsible to the BIA. They were usually "assisted" (a term that denotes the questionable relationship that has carried over into the present) by an Indian police force. The Courts of Indian Offenses were most numerous in the early 1900s, when two-thirds of all reservations were reported to have them. Throughout the course of their development, the BIA exerted a heavy influence on them.[22]

Under the impetus of the Indian Reorganization Act of 1934[23] and the deemphasis of assimilation policies, reduction of the BIA role, and increased delegation of authority to the tribes themselves, the Courts of Indian Offenses began to give way to the modern-day tribal courts. Today the Courts of Offenses have been almost completely phased out, and the tribal courts are dominant, although on a few reservations the transition either has not begun or is still in progress. The crucial aspect of this transition, theoretically if not always practically significant and salutary, is that under the tribal court system judges are

---

21. William T. Hagan, Indian Police and Judges: Experiments in Acculturation and Control (New Haven, Conn.: Yale University Press, 1966). See also Note, The Indian: The Forgotten American, 81 Harv. L. Rev. 1818, 1832 (1968), and Kerr, *supra* note 2, at 321. The history of the eastern tribes is different, however. Many disintegrated almost completely; others that survived in some form never experienced the conditions under which tribal judicial bodies or other formal institutions could be developed independently. But a few tribes, such as the Indians of New York, the Eastern Cherokees, and the Osages and the Five Civilized Tribes in Oklahoma, developed working tribal courts even before the Courts of Indian Offenses (which were *not* imposed on them) came into being. All these tribes, however, are now under state jurisdiction. The New Mexico Pueblos never had Courts of Indian Offenses either. They have been able to maintain their semireligious "traditional" courts over the centuries, although these in turn appear to have come under Spanish influence prior to the Anglo-American influx.

22. See Hagan, *supra* note 21.

23. 25 U.S.C. sec. 461 (1964).

appointed by, paid by, and responsible to the tribe (typically the tribal council) rather than to the BIA.

POLITICAL CONTEXT

The general political context in which the operations of the tribal courts must be described and assessed is one of a growing movement toward and a stridency about Indian self-rule and separation. A decade or two ago, white politicians and many Indian leaders were still talking about assimilation, termination of the reservation system, and readying the Indian for off-reservation life; today such language is political suicide. The present code words are "self-determination" and "retrocession" of landholdings, powers and rights taken from, or abandoned by, the tribes in past contacts with white society. Specifically, there is increasing support and clamor for the tribal courts to assume, to reassume, or to widen jurisdiction over matters of law and people which are currently outside their scope. The 1975 Senate hearings before the Subcommittee on Indian Affairs[24] on the Indian Law Enforcement Improvement Act of 1975 reflect the current dominance of the sovereignty-retrocession perspective and the growing suspicion and hostility with which the status of, let alone any proposal for, tribal submission to state jurisdiction is viewed.

The political state of affairs puts a special burden on this report: a portion of the readership will be looking for quick, one-dimensional answers to complex and diffuse questions; a certain percentage is likely to take offense no matter what is described or concluded; others may derive undue satisfaction from seeing their preconceived views or prejudices confirmed. I have made an assiduous effort to be neutral in both the information-gathering and the reporting processes. I have tried to seek out and give significance to the views of the Indian people themselves, and *not* just those of the political leaders or institutional officials, but also the views of people who have no political or institutional stake in these matters. I have tried to make judg-

---

24. Hearings on S.2010 Before the Subcomm. on Indian Affairs of the Senate Comm. on Interior and Insular Affairs, 94th Cong., 1st Sess. (1975-76). *Cf.* notes 6, 13, and text *supra*.

ments based on ideas of fairness which I believe are shared generally, among Indians and non-Indians, modernists or traditionalists, lawyers and nonlawyers. I have sought to avoid the paternalistic view that only white ways and institutions are desirable and relevant, as well as the opposite view that Indians ought to be left to their own devices no matter what the consequences. For example, in this report I have refrained from faulting the tribal courts for failure to meet "constitutional" requirements of providing counsel. Instead, I have made an attempt to assess whether and under what circumstances the help of counsel—professional or otherwise—would be relevant or important in the tribal court setting.

Finally, there is the problem of generalization. To generalize is always hazardous, but to avoid generalization means to avoid communication. It may be pointed out that the observations and experiences on 10 reservations cannot speak entirely satisfactorily for the situation on 60-100 other reservations. Even among the reservations visited, there are differences that defy generalization; nonetheless, a certain commonality of experience permits assessments whose applicability extends to the reservation court system in general. In any event, since this report contains much specific description to go along with its generalizations, a basis is provided for an independent judgment of the force and credibility of the broader conclusions.

RESERVATION LIFE

For the outsider visiting an Indian reservation, the first and overwhelming impression is that the living conditions and way of life are far from enviable. Most of the Indians have concentrated themselves in a number of small towns or settlements, where they live in ramshackle wooden homes or huts or, more and more these days, new cheap and sterile prefabs. Typically, the remaining stretches of reservation land—often vast areas—are unused (unusable?) and uninhabited (uninhabitable?).[25] Litter in

---

25. The "new Indian" perspective is characterized by an unrelenting desire to have it both ways. Steiner's book (*supra* note 2), for example, is filled with the kind of reasoning that on the one hand claims the reservation lands are worthless and on the other accuses whites of exploiting, or continuing to want to steal for exploitation, the

the form of useless furniture, automobile parts, even rusting hulks of abandoned cars, and other rubble often clutters the "backyards" or lines the town streets, many of which remain unpaved. Scruffy, seemingly ownerless dogs roam the streets. Often there is a small better-kept part of town with more substantial homes and watered lawns. This is where the BIA and tribal officials live, with their office buildings—often newly constructed—generally located in the same area. This is not, however, where and how the average reservation resident lives.

While some individuals and families on the reservations have retained a dignified and more or less traditional way of life, and others have made a "successful" transition to a more modern and acculturated life-style, the majority of the reservation people appear to be trapped in a cultural no-man's-land that is debilitating and demoralizing in its effect on the "inhabitants." Traditional pursuits such as hunting and fishing no longer occupy significant numbers of people. Cattle or sheep herding, farming, or working in arts and crafts sustain relatively few. The number of people who can be employed in tribal industries such as lumber or mining is limited. And while some Indians still live idealized, if subsistence, lives in individual "hogans" or communal "pueblos," many more have succumbed to the pressures of "urbanization," becoming residents of the typically drab and depressing reservation towns. Life there is sedentary and housebound; in socioeconomic terms it is at best marginal. More often than not the opportunities that still exist for living the "traditional," productive life appear to be rigorously avoided. On many reservations where the rivers and lakes are still filled with fish, one is often hard pressed to find people fishing for sport, let alone for sustenance or commerce. On another level—trivial,

---

same worthless lands. While coming close to identifying some of the real problems, Price nonetheless displays much the same mentality in the following passage:

> In Southern California, a drive from Indio to El Centro along the Salton Sea is dramatic demonstration of the special problems of Indian land. Alternate sections are Indian-held; those sections owned by non-Indians flourish with date palms, other agricultural uses, and some industrial and residential improvements, while the Indian-held land languishes in the grip of restrictive leasing policy, the ensnarlment of distrust, the heavy hand of cautious bureaucracy, and the crippling uncertainty of informal and formally conflicting claims.

Price, *supra* note 2, at 618.

but nonetheless telling—instead of walking the short distances within reservation towns that would be easy on bright winter or warm summer days, the Indians drive about in their ubiquitous pick-up trucks or in gas-guzzling, smoking old sedans.

Life on the reservations is not healthy either. Apart from the statistics on the subject, considerable evidence of alcoholism can hardly escape the most casual observer. Many Indians are afflicted with birth defects or suffer from serious dietary imbalances. With startling regularity, one sees individuals who walk with a limp or who are grossly overweight. One can detect a streak of self-destructiveness among the Indian people without having to resort to suicide statistics. In Montana, for example, where it is the lugubrious but perhaps effective practice to erect commemorative crosses along the highways at spots where car accidents have resulted in fatalities, the message hits home with the driver about every 20 or 30 miles. But near Browning, on the Blackfeet Reservation in northwestern Montana, there are stretches of road where the message comes as often as some 10 or 12 times per 20 or 30 miles—bad roads and drinking forming a lethal combination. Drinking itself is, of course, a form of self-destructiveness; for anyone who doubts that, a trip to any reservation and the surrounding towns is recommended. Many of these small towns in sparsely populated areas present scenes that are a good match for the skid-row areas of major metropolitan centers. The Navajo situation is particularly striking, since the reservation proper is dry by law. But on going into Gallup, Farmington, or any of several other border towns, one discovers that the prohibition law on the reservation is at best ineffective and probably worse—actually counterproductive—in that under these circumstances the Indians are "forced" to drive 10 to 20 miles of treacherous highway to find a bar or package store and then to drive back afterward. For those who can take their drink without frills, there is a place called the Navajo Inn only about 1.5 miles (i.e., 20 miles closer than Gallup) from Window Rock, the reservation capital, which makes up in convenience for what it lacks in class. There, at all hours of the day and night, including the middle of the afternoon in the broiling sun, people in all stages of inebriation, including stupor, wander in and out of the bar, cross the highway, stand or sit around in clumps or by themselves among the rocks and sand, or lie on the ground as if dead. Most of these people appear to be hard-core alcoholics whose lives have in large part been lived in a state of severe addiction. The Navajo tribe has tried—so far unsuccessfully—to have the place closed down, on grounds that it is a public nuisance, a health hazard, and an embarrassment to the Navajo Nation. What has been accomplished is the erection of a highway sign warning motorists euphemistically of "pedestrians"—"alcoholics crossing" is what it really means.

There are many other subtle and less subtle signs of stagnation and decay on the reservations. For those who like to rail against various "isms"—actual or imagined—it is difficult to think of a better case against "colonialism," "welfarism," or "paternalism" than the real physical and psychological plight of so many of the reservation people.

This background on reservation life is crucial for evaluating the tribal court phenomenon. The implications are various: positively, an awareness of general reservation conditions can help toward understanding court problems and solutions; negatively, it can reinforce the cycle of guilt over the origin and perpetuation of these conditions and thus block objective assessment of the courts' operations. Finally, one could dispute the negative characterization of reservation life, or challenge the right to make such an "objective" characterization. One could argue, for example, that life in many off-reservation areas is equally unappealing and that many people, though by no means all, *choose* to live where they live. Many reservation Indians in particular have tried life elsewhere—usually a big city—and having found it at least equally wanting have returned to the reservation. It is important not to ignore the subjective and relative in any talk about the quality of life. Still, from spending time on the reservations talking and dealing with the Indian people, one is struck forcibly with the impression that for many Indians—subjectively—life is unsatisfactory and unrewarding and often bleak and hopeless. The so-called objective indicators—the alcoholism, education, unemployment, health, and suicide statistics[26]—also speak subjectively.

---

26. Despite the fact that all kinds of numbers are continually and liberally thrown about, reliable vital statistics for the total Indian population of the United States are

THE COURTS: GENERAL DESCRIPTION

A general overview of the tribal courts will set the tone and provide a context for the more detailed material to be presented later.

Procedure

Obviously, there are some noticeable differences in procedure and decorum among the courts of different reservations, as there are differences in style and personality among the various tribal judges. And to some extent, such disparities reflect the status of the various courts, their level of performance, their reputation, and their self-concept.

On one of the smaller reservations, for example, the tribal chief justice could be found during office hours lounging around in street clothes with his feet propped up on his desk, on which prominently displayed was the sign, Come on In; Everything

---

hard to come by. A recent booklet disseminated by the Recruitment Leadership and Training Institute (U.S. Office of Education) listed the following up-to-date information to support its objectives:

> The average life expectancy of the Native American is estimated anywhere between 44 and 66.5 years. The national [non-Indian] figure is 70.4. [Is there any meaning in estimates that present such an enormous range?]
>
> Infant mortality is twice the national average.
>
> The average annual income for Native-American families has been estimated at $1,150 for those living on reservations.
>
> The unemployment rate for Native Americans is 40% with an additional 19% working in temporary or seasonal jobs.
>
> The suicide rate is 21.8 per 100,000 as compared with the national rate of 11.3 per 100,000.
>
> Dropout rates among Indian children were twice the national average in both public and Federal schools with some school districts having rates [of] approximately 100%.
>
> Achievement levels of Indian children were two to three years below those of white students and Indian children fell progressively further behind the longer they stayed in school.

Bridging the Gap: Recruiting Indian People for Careers in Education (Philadelphia: Recruitment Leadership and Training Institute, n.d.), passim.

There have been numerous nonnational assessments of the severity of alcohol problems among the Indians. See, e.g., Robert A. Fairbanks, The Cheyenne-Arapaho and Alcoholism: Does the Tribe Have a Legal Right to a Medical Remedy? 1 Am. Indian L. Rev. 55 (1973). In the introductory paragraph, Fairbanks reports that "nearly 75 percent of the approximately 4,000 remaining [Cheyenne-Arapaho] tribal members have alcohol problems of some nature." See also Steiner, supra note 2, for a variety of statistics. Several of the judges on the reservations I studied freely—indeed with a measure of pride—disclosed that they were reformed alcoholics.

Else Has Gone Wrong. Even on the bench, robeless still, the judge affected the same air of informality and accessibility. Certainly, this posture was consistent with the tone of informality and often lighthearted (but one suspects, somewhat desperate) cynicism that pervaded most reservation affairs. At the other extreme, the chief judge of the Navajo tribal court seemed to be engaged in a deliberate attempt to create the opposite effect; when presiding, he and his associates were fully robed; when not, they were dressed in gray business suits. The air of formality in the Navajo courts was in sharp contrast with the atmosphere on the other reservation. But it is difficult to say what these differences in style mean or which style is preferable. Is the remoteness and formality of the one court more appropriate and effective than the extreme casualness of the other? Does it depend on the "culture" of the particular reservation, on what the people expect? *What* do they, or have they been led to, expect? It is probably better to save one's analysis for more concrete things. Many basic similarities among the reservations and their courts outweigh the smaller differences.

Legal Code

In all the tribal courts, the applicable law is the tribal code of the reservation. However, the term "tribal code" is not to be taken as indicating that the law is indigenously or traditionally Indian or that its designation as the code of reservation X necessarily means that it is different in origin and content than the code of reservation Y. Instead, the reservation codes are versions of old BIA codes and models that have undergone some localized updatings at the hands of tribal attorneys, regional BIA personnel, and/or professors from nearby universities (non-Indian all) who—occasionally with some input from tribal (Indian) judges or council members—have put together these curious but unquestionably Anglo-American documents. Mixed in with the BIA-derived laws are usually some elements of state law and state or federal constitutional provisions; occasionally one can find something with Indian roots, like a criminal prohibition against "malicious gossip" (e.g., in the Blackfeet code). Despite its apparent operational inefficacy, a prohibition against the use of alcohol remains in the codes of some of the tribes. Typically, the codes exhibit substantial gaps, to be filled in by state law (as some of the codes explicitly provide) when the situation arises. However, lack of legal training and high turnover among tribal judges mean that many judges are unfamiliar with the code itself, let alone the state law that is supposed to complement it. On most reservations, the codes exist in mimeographed, unbound, or loose-leaf form. But there are exceptions. On the Navajo Reservation the tribal code is bound in two hard-cover volumes that are indistinguishable from the statutory material found in any legal library. Also, although the practice is becoming less exceptional as other "progressive" reservations do the same, the Navajo court puts great emphasis on expanding and revising the code—in fact one gets the impression of a somewhat unmanageable proliferation of new "tribal" law—and unlike the average reservation court, the Navajo court has a sizable library stocked with state and federal statutes and case reports.

Personnel

Lack of legally trained personnel is a pervasive characteristic that extends to all parts of the tribal law-and-order system. Tribal judges are usually Indians from the local reservation. Occasionally, they are picked from the ranks of the tribal police. They may have some political prominence, but their educational qualifications are rarely a consideration. It is therefore exceptional for a tribal judge to have a formal education beyond the level of that of the average reservation resident (i.e., the high school level, if that). Efforts to train tribal judges once they are appointed began about six years ago under the auspices of the National American Indian Court Judges Association. These efforts, the aim and relevance of which are not always clear, suffer especially from the turnover problem mentioned above. On many reservations, tribal judges are appointed for short terms of only two to four years, and owing to periodic political upheavals in which they are often among the casualties, they in fact serve even shorter terms. Such discontinuity frustrates many of the legal training efforts and precludes the accumulation of practical experience in the tribal courts. On a few reservations, white lawyers from the surrounding area have been recruited to sit on the tribal court for all cases; in others, for only the legally complex or the politically sensitive ones. In terms of promoting objective and professional justice, the visiting-judge system has a good deal to recommend it, but the "logic" of the tribal court system, as well as the present trend toward self-determination on the reservations, seems to preclude its extensive adoption. Precisely for these reasons, in fact, at least one such judge (at Standing Rock) was being "phased out."

About the only people connected with the tribal courts who have formal legal training are the (typically non-Indian) "legal advisors" employed by a few of the courts (e.g., Blackfeet, Navajo). While they perform some useful functions for the courts, these recent law school graduates tend to become involved in matters that are basically political and well beyond their legal expertise and general experience. Partly as a result, the turnover rate among them is very high. On one reservation, the longevity "record" for legal advisors was reported to be seven months.

On many reservations there is no tribal prosecutor; where there is one, he, like the tribal judge, is likely to be a local Indian resident without legal training. At least one court, the Uintah and Ouray, brings in an associate from a Salt Lake City law firm to act as prosecutor in contested criminal cases. In the absence of a prosecutor, the tribal judge or a member of the police force, or both, assume the prosecutorial role. This situation is frequently perceived as threatening the impartiality of the judge. Tribal policemen, even though they have the charge of "lack of professionalism" leveled at them most frequently and from all angles, actually have no less, and sometimes more, training than other law-and-order functionaries. A good percentage have attended police academies for at least some time. The utility of the training no doubt varies with the academy, with the individual, and with the time spent. Moreover, politics and other incidents of reservation life also take their toll of the tribal police, and turnover is another problem.

The situation with regard to defense counsel in tribal courts is a mixture of real needs and partial or inapposite responses to them. Typically, the "tribal attorneys" (almost invariably white) represent the interests of the tribe only; they do not represent the concerns of individual Indians in the tribal courts. On a few reservations, government-funded lawyers may be available to individuals. On others, local private attorneys may handle individual casework in the tribal courts. On the whole, however, the appearance of professional attorneys in tribal courts is kept to a minimum. Many tribal codes have or once had provisions that explicitly prohibited the appearance of professional lawyers in the courts. Since the passage of the Indian Civil Rights Act in 1968, one provision of which is that no Indian tribe shall deny to a person in a criminal proceeding the right to counsel at his own expense,[27] these prohibitions may no longer be in the codes, or if still in, they are open to challenge. Regardless of the interpretation given to this civil rights provision, many tribal officials—especially court personnel—are determined to see to it that the appearance of professional lawyers in the reservation courts remains a rarity.

With the help of legal consultants, some tribes have set up tribal bar examinations. The underlying objective of these barriers to practice in the tribal courts appears to be the assertion of tribal sovereignty and separatism. Also operative may be the fear that nontribal attorneys will overwhelm the judges. Whatever the tribal motives, few local attorneys view these tribal bar examinations as legitimate in substance, and some refuse to take the examinations as a matter of principle.

On a number of reservations, local Indians serve as lay representatives for litigants in the tribal court. The Navajo even have a fairly extensive and organized lay-advocate system. (A possible interpretation of the Indian Civil Rights Act provision on right to counsel is that it can be satisfied by such lay representation.)[28] The performance of these lay advocates varies greatly in quantity, quality, and style.

Very few Indians in the country have graduated from law school and been admitted to a state bar: a year or two ago the total estimate stood at about 85.[29] Prospects for a dramatic increase in the coming years are said to be good. A major problem from the point of view of the tribal courts, however, is that so many Indian lawyers wind up working in the big cities. Even when they return to the reservations, Indian attorneys are likely

---

27. 25 U.S.C. sec. 1302 (6) (1970).
28. But see Turner v. American Bar Association, 407 F. Supp. 451 (N.D. Tex. 1975) and Gordon v. Justice Court, 525 P.2d 72 (1974) to the opposite effect.
29. Cf. Robert L. Knauss, Developing a Representative Legal Profession, 62 A.B.A.J. 591 (1976), particularly the table at 594. In May 1978 the Journal (64 A.B.A.J. 662) cited a current estimate of 400 "Indian lawyers."

to become involved in tribal concerns that will preclude them from representing individuals in the tribal courts.

Language

Proceedings in the tribal courts on most reservations are held in English. This may be viewed as indicative of the degree of acculturation on even the less acculturated reservations—those with tribal courts as opposed to those under state jurisdiction. On most reservations, despite recent efforts at cultural revival, the younger generations of Indians do not speak the tribal language. Occasionally, however, in tribal courts where English is the rule, an older full-blood from a remote part of the reservation may suddenly lapse into the tribal language. The judge, if able, will then respond in kind. On a few of the most traditional reservations—primarily in the Southwest—the tribal language is still a dominant force and may, for reasons of cultural assertion as much as for practicality, be the official language of the tribal court.

Facilities

Physical facilities for the reservation courts are invariably modest but usually not inadequate. New, if unspectacular, "law-and-order" buildings are a common sight. These buildings typically house the judicial offices and police quarters side by side; this situation is frequently found in white systems, but in the eyes of many reservation Indians this proximity creates an excessive "law-and-order" identification for judges already beset by the problem of overfamiliarity with—if not outright assumption of—the prosecutorial role and, in some cases, the fact of a police background. On a few of the materially less fortunate reservations, an ancient building with a dark and cramped jail still furnishes the setting for the activities of the tribal court; or an old school house, a vacated welfare office, or trailer home may be used, if not by the main court, then often by one of the branch courts on reservations where such exist. These, however, are exceptions.

Lack of clerical and technical support and absence of dispositional facilities are also common characteristics of the tribal law-and-order systems. These shortcomings, coupled with insufficient respect for the tribal judge and his own lack of authority, sometimes lead to the orders of the court simply being ignored.

Appeals

Theoretically, there is an appeals procedure within the tribal court system. The process, however, is only barely implemented. Reports of over a decade ago (1961) show only 28 appeals for *all* reservation courts during that year.[30] More recent statistics show some, but insufficient, improvement. A recent study[31] cited "fewer than 10" appeals per year (the mid-1970s) for the Blackfeet court, which has a first-instance caseload of some 4,000.[32] For the Standing Rock court, the study counted 4 appeals during the first half of 1976; for the Uintah and Ouray court there were no appeals at all during 1975.[33] No statistics were available for appeals on the Fort Totten Reservation, but the situation in this regard is given in the descriptive discussion ahead (pp. 117-19). Only the Navajo court reported a "significant" number of appeals—76 in 1974—but these were out of a total caseload of over 30,000.[34] In the Navajo system appeal means de novo review. Its nature in other tribal courts is less clear. Often there is no separate appellate body at all, but the trial judges, excluding the one who handled the original case, may perform the appellate function. There is some talk about, but few actual instances of, intertribal and interband judicial exchanges or circuit riding for appeals purposes. Appeal to the federal courts is possible on constitutional issues. This procedure has been strengthened and broadened by interpretations of the Indian Civil Rights Act and is being used with greater frequency,

---

30. See, e.g., Senate hearings report, *supra* note 2, at 751-52 n.1, for the extremely low number of appeals for each area office. See also *id.* at 140, 146, 153-56, 163, 208, & 209.

31. Indian Self-Determination and the Role of the Tribal Courts: A Survey of Tribal Courts Conducted by the American Indian Lawyer Training Program [Washington, D.C.: Bureau of Indian Affairs, 1977] [hereinafter cited as AILTP survey].

32. The total caseload figures were collected as part of this study. See their examination below at pp. 28-42.

33. See notes 31, 32 *supra*.

34. Both the appeals and total caseload figures come from the Navajo court's annual report for 1974.

although it remains, of course, an exceptional event in the total flow of cases.

Tribal Politics

To give a comprehensive and realistic picture of first-instance reservation justice, one must deal with the problem of reservation politics. This is a broad and fuzzy topic that elicits much feeling. Although impressions abound, there is little hard evidence on the subject. That does not make the politics any less real or significant. The political realities cannot be ignored. The consensus is (and from field experience I concur) that lack of training and politics are the major obstacles faced by tribal judges in their efforts to dispense justice. The two factors are in some ways connected. On the reservations, already seriously lacking in forceful and capable leadership (the reservation setting seldom breeds such people, and those it produces often leave), political events conspire toward keeping those few who do have relevant qualities and qualifications away from the tribal judge positions.

Selection of Judges

By and large, the most able people do not want to be judges, would seldom get the job even if they wanted it, and stand a good chance of not keeping it if, against the odds, they do get it. The position of tribal judge has neither a high status nor a high salary, and it has the potential for creating many enemies on the closed and factionalized reservations. Tribal judges are paid between $9,000 and $11,000 a year, which often is not competitive with the salaries of comparable or less responsible tribal or government positions. On most reservations, the tribal council appoints the judges; in a few cases, the BIA still plays a role, for example, by retaining the power of approval over a list of candidates or over the final nominees themselves. Apparently, the councils do not invariably resist the temptation to appoint politically weak and manipulable judges. On a minority of reservations, popular election of tribal judges is the rule. This system has the theoretical advantage of reducing the possibility of tribal council control. As a practical matter, however, the popular election system does not appear to work well. Until 1960 the

Navajo operated with a popularly elected court, under which
system the court fell apart completely.[35] Reports from other
reservations also indicate that the election system is not successful in shielding the judge from council influence. In addition, an
elective judiciary raises the potentiality that the judges will be
perpetually running for office. When asked about the alternative
of popular election on a reservation where the council appoints,
a former judge of the Standing Rock tribal court responded:
"No, it won't work. They'd [the judges] just be trying to keep
the vote. There's too much clannishness on the reservation. You
find one person guilty and you've gotten 20 relatives mad and
lost 20 votes." Not the kind of "responsiveness to the people"
that is meant by the concept of popular election.

Status of Judges

Interviews with reservation people reveal a low level of respect
for and confidence in the tribal judges. Lack of legal knowledge
is an often-cited criticism. In addition, there are widespread alle-
gations of judicial favoritism toward council members who have
been charged with criminal offenses as well as frequent charges
of council interference in judicial decisions that do not directly
involve matters or individuals related to the council. Other complaints about the partiality of judges and speculations about
their motivations also crop up. For example, a judge from the
South Dakota part of the Standing Rock Reservation was
accused of never convicting anyone from his part of the reservation. Judged by the frequency of stories about it, favoritism to
council members was seen as an especially big problem on the
Standing Rock, Uintah and Ouray, and Blackfeet reservations,
although it is impossible to substantiate the charges. Tribal
governments have no tradition of separation of powers. But this
does not prevent many reservation residents, some reform-
oriented Indian leaders, and even some of the tribal judges themselves from seeing political and social influence in judicial affairs
generally, and council interference specifically, as one of the
main problems on the reservations.

---

35. This, at least, is the assessment of the chief justice of the current appointive
system. It may be somewhat self-serving.

Political infighting and factionalism are said to be a way of life on the reservations. Political power changes hands frequently, and council members and chairmen come and go in rapid succession. Elections are not only hotly contested but lengthily disputed as well. Charges of fraud reverberate long after the results are in, and some wind up as acrimonious cases in the tribal or federal courts.[36] One by-product of this political instability is its effect on judicial personnel (as well as on other law enforcement officials, such as chiefs of police or even lower-echelon officers). Tribal judges are not only at the mercy of one council (or a constant constituency of council members) but, in addition, may be victims of the spoils system when the council is ousted or when power within it changes hands. There are some exceptions. The judges of the Navajo Reservation are now appointed for life,[37] and in the early summer of 1975, it was pointed out with pride that 3 of the 7 judges had experience ranging from 6 to 15 years on the tribal bench. Unfortunately, a few months later 2 of the 3 experienced judges resigned and another judge quit, destroying much of what had been achieved along these lines. Political and financial factors appear to have figured prominently in this sudden exodus of judicial personnel, which, along with resignations in prosecutor, defense, and police departments, left the whole Navajo system of justice in disarray. The fact that one judge left to take another tribal government job and another resigned to set himself up as a used-car salesman only added insult to injury. The chief judges on the Blackfeet and Uintah and Ouray reservations each have about 10 years of experience, but their associate judges have little or none. Chief judges and associates on Stand-

---

36. A significant number of cases in the federal reports are on the subject of tribal election disputes. Some recent examples are: White Eagle v. One Feather, 478 F.2d 1311 (8th Cir. 1973); Daly v. United States, 483 F.2d 700 (8th Cir. 1973); Barrackman v. Artichoker, Civil No. 71-386 (D. Arizona, Jan. 16, 1973); Armstrong v. Howard, Civil No. 6-72-315 (D. Minn., Nov. 16, 1972); MacKay v. Lummi Business Council, Civil No. 20-72 C2 (W.D. Wash., June 29, 1972); McCurdy v. Steele, 353 F. Supp. 629 (D. Utah, 1973); and St. Marks v. Canaan, Civil No. 2928 (D. Mont., Oct. 23, 1970).

37. The lifetime appointment scheme is accompanied by a provision that newly appointed judges shall serve the first two years on probationary status. While it has obvious merit, such a provision also creates the possibility of political abuse.

ing Rock and Fort Totten follow the typical pattern: they come and go more quickly than one can keep track of.

An illustration from the Blackfeet Reservation sums up the problems of personnel and politics: following a series of resignations, the tribal council duly appointed a search committee to select candidates for five vacant judgeships. After two months of operation, the committee had yet to find one candidate willing and able to serve.

Training of Judges

The training program sponsored by the National American Indian Court Judges Association faces some very fundamental difficulties. How does one train these judges who have so little overall education? What does one train them in? What does one train them for? Who should do the training? These questions have no ready answers. Given the gaps in the tribal judges' backgrounds and the gaps in knowledge about what it takes to be a good judge or to train one, wherever he may be functioning, a sense of futility about the program is unavoidable.

A sketch of one of the training sessions I attended helps illustrate the difficulties. Typically, this particular two-day session was held at an airport hotel in a centrally located city, Denver. Some 150 tribal judges and associate judges came to listen to 4 lecturers who held sessions simultaneously throughout the day before groups of 30-40. On the first day, attentiveness was pretty good; on the second both attentiveness and attendance waned significantly. One Indian judge who had been through several sessions over the past couple of years said that he "used to fall asleep all the time, but now they're beginning to be pretty interesting, you know." When asked if they considered the sessions helpful, most of the judges responded in the affirmative. A few judges were drunk throughout the training period. These reactions were not too different from those one might expect at any other convention or workshop. The "gap" that existed, however, between teachers and trainees and between authors and readers of the written training materials was of a special dimension.

Although it varied in intensity with the particular speaker and the subject treated, a special communication problem was always there. For example, a lecture on family law and child welfare given by a white psychologist who indulged in frequent moralisms and quoted dubious statistics on the national incidence of incest produced some laughter and "amens" from the Indian judges, who saw in it a confirmation of the decadence of white society, but otherwise yielded little of educational value. Another session on preventive social work by a white social worker resulted in more serious participation, but much of the educational message was lost when two female tribal judges instigated a bitter personal-political reaction that terminated in the social worker's being charged with racism and reduced to tears. Yet another lecture on delinquency jurisdiction by a white juvenile court judge got hopelessly bogged down in simplistic talk and political arguments concerning Indian sovereignty, which shed little light on an essentially difficult conceptual and practical topic. Training manuals circumvent the problems of personal reaction and digression, but that in itself hardly guarantees the suitability of the material. It is doubtful, for example, that the 90-page *Criminal Court Procedure Manual* and its 176-page supporting *Research Document,* which cover subjects from "free exercise of religion" to "bills of attainder and ex post facto laws," are very useful to the tribal judges, some of whom can barely read or write and many of whom have only very limited experience as judges.

The above is not to say that formal (legal) training is an unnecessary asset for a tribal judge; to the contrary, it is essential. Can one, however, expect it to be acquired by the current crop of tribal judges? It may well be that this is expecting too much of both educator and trainee. The job of educating is not that simple; the job of judging is not that simple. Often the problems brought into the tribal courts, while technically not "major," are nonetheless serious and complex—factually, legally, and sociologically. They are complicated by peculiar jurisdictional uncertainties, tribal factionalism, and a cultural situation that appears to work against the Indians' understanding and accepting the legal process. The sometimes-expressed idea that dispensing justice in this setting requires only a dose of "natural wisdom" is not tenable. Few persons would indulge in such romanticism in relation to the dispensing of justice in non-Indian society.[38] Why it should hold for tribal justice needs explanations that have not been, and are not likely to be, forthcoming.

STATISTICS ON CRIMES AND DISPUTES

The rates for illegal activity (criminal or civil) on the reservations are less known and less frequently cited than other vital statistics.[39] That crime is a serious problem on most reservations is acknowledged by people from every group and faction—whether reservation residents or outsiders, "experts" or casual observers, Indians or whites. Putting the problem in an accurate and a comparatively meaningful context is more difficult. Reliable statistics are simply not available. Beyond that, to assert that crime is a "serious problem" or that civil disputes are common implies—somewhat too hopefully—that there is some agreement about the number and relative seriousness of the offenses, some consistency in reporting and categorizing, and some consensus on whether to compare the reservation population with off-reservation Indians, with non-Indians in rural areas surrounding the reservations, or with urban residents.

Available statistics from the reservations can provide a rough indication of the magnitude of the problems. But it must be stressed that one must exercise considerable caution in interpreting them. The schemes used to classify and report crimes and disputes are only marginally comparable from reservation to reservation, or even within one reservation from year to year.

Criminal statistics for the years 1970-72 for Standing Rock Reservation (population 4,460-6,000) are shown in table 1.[40]

---

38. The law review literature, for example, on the use of lay judges in white courts tends to be extremely critical of such surviving practices. See, e.g., Note, Limiting Judicial Incompetence: The Due Process Right to a Legally Learned Judge in State Minor Court Criminal Proceedings, 61 Va. L. Rev. 1454 (1975); Note, The "Right" to a Neutral and Competent Judge in Ohio's Mayor's Court, 36 Ohio St. L.J. 889 (1975). See also Comment, The Justice of the Peace System under Constitutional Attack—*Gordon v. Justice Court*, 1974 Utah L. Rev. 861; and Gordon v. Justice Court, 12 Cal. 3d 323, 525 P.2d 72 (1974), and Turner v. American Bar Association, 407 F. Supp. 451 (N.D. Tex., 1975).

39. Cf. note 26 supra.

40. The Standing Rock statistics, like the Blackfeet statistics, are from standard reporting forms collected locally by the BIA, and were obtained locally. My efforts to obtain statistics through regional or national BIA channels were fruitless.

No figures on civil cases could be obtained for this study. However, a more recent survey[41] counts 333 "civil" cases for the year 1975. Lest this be viewed as evidence of a substantial civil component to the Standing Rock court's work, it should be noted that this count is composed mostly of juvenile cases that are mainly criminal. The "civil" figure should also be contrasted with the enormous (adult) criminal caseload.

For the Blackfeet Reservation (population slightly over 6,000) only the 1973 criminal statistics could be obtained (see table 2).[42]

Statistics for the Navajo Reservation (population between 100,000 and 146,000)[43] are recorded and reported under a different system. The 1974 figures for both criminal and civil cases were made available and are shown in table 3.

The dispositional pattern in the Navajo courts had to be pieced together from unprocessed raw court data. A compilation of criminal case records covering two quarters of the calendar year 1975 (January-June) showed that, of the total persons charged, 89.4 percent were found guilty and 5.3 percent were either acquitted or dismissed. One might conjecture that the remaining 5.3 percent that were unaccounted for were informal dismissals or possibly included unrecorded guilty findings or pleas as well.

For the Devil's Lake, Fort Totten, and Uintah and Ouray reservations very little in the way of statistics was obtained. From a variety of secondary sources[44] it can be gathered that the total tribal criminal court caseload at Fort Totten (population about 1,500-2,000) was 403 in 1960 and 439 in 1961.[45]

For the Uintah and Ouray Reservation (population about

---

41. The AILTP survey, *supra* note 31.

42. The AILTP survey (*supra* note 31) counts 7,000 total cases for the Blackfeet court for 1975. Of these, 70 percent are reported to be criminal; 10 percent, traffic; and the remaining 20 percent, juvenile, small claims, or other civil matters.

43. See *infra* note 76 and text accompanying.

44. E.g., the Senate hearings report, *supra* note 2, app. H, at 247-50.

45. A recent newspaper report concerning the distribution of the $8.35 million received in a land settlement between the tribe and the U.S. government gave 2,673 as the number of enrolled tribal members of the Devil's Lake Tribe (Chicago Sun-Times, Jan. 3, 1978, at 4, col. 1). However, many of the enrolled members do not live on the reservation. For some, the status and activities as tribal members probably stop at their being claimants in a distribution of money.

TABLE 1   "Crime" Figures for Standing Rock Reservation, 1970-72

A. No. of Offenses Reported or Known to Police and No. Cleared by Arrests

No. of Offenses

	1970		1971		1972	
	Reported or Known to Police	Cleared by Arrests	Reported or Known to Police	Cleared by Arrests	Reported or Known to Police	Cleared by Arrests
Criminal homicide	5	5	1	1	3	3
Forcible rape	5	5	3	3	1	1
Robbery	1	1	0	0	0	0
Assault	10	10	8	8	4	4
Burglary	8	6	9	9	7	5
Larceny	1	1	1	1	0	0
Auto theft	0	0	0	0	0	0
Arson	0	0	0	0	2	2
Forgery-Counterfeiting	0	0	0	0	0	0
Fraud	0	0	0	0	0	0
Embezzlement	0	0	0	0	0	0
Stolen property	0	0	0	0	0	0
Vandalisms	128	61	85	68	80	67
Weapons	20	12	21	16	16	12
Prostitution and commercial vice	0	0	0	0	0	0
Sex offenses except forcible rape and prostitution	0	0	0	0	0	0
Narcotics	0	0	0	0	2	2
Gambling	0	0	0	0	0	0

TABLE 1—continued

| | No. of Offenses | | | | | |
| | 1970 | | 1971 | | 1972 | |
	Reported or Known to Police	Cleared by Arrests	Reported or Known to Police	Cleared by Arrests	Reported or Known to Police	Cleared by Arrests
Offenses against family and children	79	58	106	101	126	119
Driving while intoxicated (d.w.i.)	11	10	88	84	39	36
Liquor laws	26	23	135	134	23	23
Drunkenness	235	206	1,314	1,242	227	221
Disorderly conduct	380	316	15	15	543	521
Vagrancy	0	0	0	0	1	0
All other offenses	965	684	1,518	1,327	554	484
Traffic except d.w.i.	98	72	96	89	79	74
Total	1,972	1,470	3,400	3,098	1,707	1,574

B. Dispositions of Criminal Caseload, Standing Rock Reservation, 1972

	No.
Total no. persons charged	1,626a
Total no. persons guilty	1,297
Acquitted or dismissed	67
Referred to juvenile court	225
Pending or prosecuted elsewhere	37

aThe total of "persons charged" (1,626) exceeds the number of "offenses" cleared by "arrest" (1,574) for the year 1972, which is not impossible, but decidedly improbable.

1,800) the total criminal caseload in the court was 542 in 1960, 697 in 1961, and 549 in 1969.[46]

The first conclusion that springs to mind from a look at these

TABLE 2   "Crime" Figures for Blackfeet Reservation, 1973

A. No. of Offenses Reported or Known to Police and No. Cleared by Arrest

	No. of Offenses	
	Reported or Known to Police	Cleared by Arrests
Criminal homicide	4	2
Forcible rape	4	3
Robbery	0	0
Assault	264	243
Burglary	104	18
Larceny	123	39
Auto theft	12	3
Arson	0	0
Forgery-Counterfeiting	19	9
Fraud	36	36
Embezzlement	3	3
Stolen property	14	0
Vandalism	29	3
Weapons	17	5
Prostitution and commercial vice	0	0
Sex offenses except forcible rape and prostitution	0	0
Narcotics	2	2
Gambling	1	1
Offenses against family and children	52	52
Driving while intoxicated (d.w.i.)	125	105
Liquor laws	73	56
Drunkenness	87	87
Disorderly conduct	1,574	1,458
Vagrancy	0	0
All other offenses	783	671
Traffic except d.w.i.	1,162	1,047
Total	4,488	3,843

B. Disposition of Criminal Caseload, Blackfeet Reservation, 1973

	No.
Total no. persons charged	3,319
Total no. persons guilty	2,081
Acquitted or dismissed	572
Referred to juvenile court	662
Pending or prosecuted elsewhere	4

---

46. See pp. 50 *infra,* for a presentation of case dispositions from the Uintah and Ouray court. The AILTP survey reports 1,500 cases for 1975, "over 1,400" of which are criminal.

statistics is that they fully confirm the impression that there is a
lot of crime (or trouble) on the reservations. The phenomenal
"crime" rates range from 25,000 to 65,000 per 100,000 inhabi-

TABLE 3   Cases "Filed and Disposed of" in the Navajo Tribal
Courts, 1974

	No.
Crimes against the person (primarily assault and battery)	1,681
Crimes against property	294
Livestock, grazing, and fencing violations	41
Offenses against family and children	354
Offenses against the public peace	10,040
Sexual misconduct	133
Liquor violations (except d.w.i.)	1,638
Driving while intoxicated (d.w.i.)	2,326
Traffic offenses (except d.w.i.)	9,387
"Other offenses"	363
Total	26,257
Total juvenile cases	2,633
Total civil cases	1,504
Grand Total	30,394

tants. To put it in even more staggering perspective: the number
of arrests on the Blackfeet Reservation in 1973 and on the
Standing Rock Reservation in 1972 well exceeded half their
respective total populations. Even recognizing that the figures
include multiple arrests for some individuals (the precise numbers for which are unknown), it remains a startling bit of testimony about one aspect of reservation life. Table 4 below com-
pares United States crime rates with those of the reservations.

The comparative figures thus reveal the "crime" level on the
reservations to be astonishingly higher than the rates in the
society at large (anywhere from 5 to more than 30 times higher,
depending on reservation, year, and demographic frame of reference—rural or both urban and rural). The magnitude of the differences leads to any of several—not mutually exclusive—conclusions: (1) such statistics cannot possibly be meaningful; (2) such
statistics must mean something; or (3) such statistics really bring
the point home about the seriousness of crime on the reservations. Which one of, or which combination of, these conclusions
one prefers or prefers to emphasize depends on one's affinity for
statistics, the strength of one's skepticism, and the limits and
directions of one's imagination generally. A closer look at the
figures also helps.

It stands out immediately that on the Standing Rock and Blackfeet reservations a huge chunk of the caseload is in the categories of "drunkenness" and/or "disorderly conduct." In fact, much of what shows up as drunkenness on Standing Rock is apparently treated as disorderly conduct by the Blackfeet system. On the Navajo Reservation, "offenses against the public peace"—of which there were a very high 10,040 in 1974—apparently take the place of the drunk-disorderly charges. That these crime categories are virtually interchangeable is a fact that holds for nonreservation law enforcement as well. The

TABLE 4   Total Estimated Arrests, with Rates per 100,000 Population

	No. of Arrests	Rate per 100,000 Overall	Rural Areas
United States:			
1974	9,055,800	4,584	2,758
1970	8,117,700	4,288	1,993
Standing Rock:			
1971	3,098	56,327	
1972	1,574	28,618	
Blackfeet	3,843	64,050	
Navajo, 1974	28,890	24,075	
Uintah & Ouray, 1969 .	549	30,500	
Fort Totten, 1961	439	29,267	

Source: The United States figures are from Crime in the United States: Uniform Crime Reports, 1970, 1974 (Washington, D.C.: Federal Bureau of Investigation, 1971, 1975). Their label as estimates acknowledges the reality of imprecision. The U.S. figures do not include traffic arrests, which are part of the reservation totals. On the other hand, categories such as curfew and loitering law violations and runaway arrests, appearing in the U.S. statistics, are not found in the reservation totals. If one finds it more meaningful, one can recompute the comparative rates after subtracting the traffic cases from the reservation totals. The total populations of the reservations have, for purposes of these computations, been assumed to be set at 5,500, 6,000, 120,000, 1,800, and 1,500 for the Standing Rock, Blackfeet, Navajo, Uintah and Ouray, and Fort Totten reservations, respectively.

The Navajo, Uintah and Ouray, and Fort Totten figures are court caseload totals rather than arrests. The number of arrests is normally higher than the court caseload as a result of screening by police and prosecutor agencies. On the reservations, however, such screening is minimal. As noted above, the Standing Rock court caseload actually exceeds the total number of arrests. The Blackfeet court caseload is some 13 percent less than the arrest volume. Disparities in either direction appear as likely to be statistical or administrative errors as the result of decision making on some rational and conscious level.

unusually high number of drunkenness arrests on Standing Rock in 1971 as compared with 1970 and 1972 is interesting but not easy to explain. Partly, there was a trade-off with "disorderly" arrests, which were unusually low during 1971. It also appears, however, that in 1971 law-enforcement policy makers decided to crack down (or at least begin reporting as if they were cracking down) on public alcohol-related misbehavior. The unusually high number of "liquor law violations" and "other offenses" furnishes supporting evidence for that supposition. In 1972, "crime" on Standing Rock (i.e., law enforcement and reporting) returned to "normal."

A number of inferences can be drawn from the high volume of arrests and charges for drunkenness-related disturbances on the reservations. The most obvious one is that it is inevitable in settings where the incidence of alcoholism and the unemployment rates are high and where income is low. Beyond that, there is room for some more discriminating speculation. On each of the reservations visited, the tribal judges or reservation residents complained that the tribal police habitually made arrests and filed charges with the court when they could have easily handled the situation without such formal processing. In other words, it is likely that the drunkenness problem and the total crime picture on the reservations is distorted or inflated by overzealousness on the part of the tribal police in certain kinds of cases. Counterbalancing this possibility, however, is the allegation that the police fail to do the job in various other—and often more serious—categories of cases. There are some indications of this effect in the statistics, particularly those from the Blackfeet Reservation. The disparity between "offenses reported or known to the police"[47] and "offenses cleared by arrests" is quite high in such categories as burglary, larceny, weapons, and auto theft. Some of this can be attributed to jurisdictional uncertainties: neither the tribal police nor the FBI is willing or able to accept responsibility in cases that can be classified as either felonies ("major" crimes) or misdemeanors, thus falling on either side of the dividing line between federal and tribal jurisdiction. Other

---

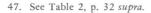

47. See Table 2, p. 32 *supra*.

reasons for failing to arrest some serious offenders include lack of manpower and lack of skill on the part of the tribal police. In addition, in some cases the police have allegedly been deliberately inactive as a result of political disputes within the tribe or between the tribe and "outside" agencies. It is difficult to confirm such charges, but these various possibilities should be considered in trying to understand the crime picture on the reservations.

The statistics also reveal a high volume of crimes against the person. In 1974 such crimes (numbering 1,681) made up the third-highest category of offenses on the Navajo Reservation. The 243 assaults on the Blackfeet Reservation also indicate a serious level of interpersonal violence. It is not known how much other crime against persons may be hidden in the impersonal drunkenness and disorderly or "public peace" categories. On Standing Rock, there are comparatively low totals for assault, but this is probably a matter of the reporters' relegating such offenses to alternative categories. Cases observed in the Standing Rock court and sketches of reservation life given by Standing Rock informants suggest that interpersonal violence growing out of drinking bouts is as common there as on other reservations.

Numerically, "offenses against family and children" make up a comparatively significant class of offenses on the reservations. These offenses include parental neglect, nonsupport, and "illicit cohabitation," problems to which alcoholism and the economic precariousness of reservation life often contribute.

Alcoholism also plays a major role in traffic violations. Driving while intoxicated—a frequent cause for arrest—is the most obvious and serious drinking-related traffic offense. Alcohol figures in many other moving violations—reckless driving and the like—as well. Nonmoving violations revolve around lack of a valid driver's license, or defects in the vehicles driven. The tribal judges indicate that many reservation residents are only marginally aware of the need for such formalities as licenses, while others simply prefer to avoid the trouble of obtaining one. Some individuals may have had their licenses suspended or confiscated as a result of previous violations, although the evidence (furnished by the judges themselves) is that the punitive taking of licenses is an infrequent practice—probably too infrequent.

Vehicles with defective equipment of various kinds are a common problem, as revealed by simple observation. One peculiarity in the pattern of traffic problems is the extremely low volume of traffic arrests on the Standing Rock Reservation as compared with the Blackfeet and Navajo picture. Again, it is safe to assume that this is a matter of differential enforcement and reporting rather than an actual difference in driving or licensing behavior. Accounts from a Standing Rock tribal judge and several other informants, observations in court and on the roads, the fact that driving-while-intoxicated arrests are much closer to "par," all provide evidence that traffic is no less a problem on Standing Rock than on the other reservations.

On the reservations, one finds relatively few crimes against property and little forgery-fraud-embezzlement, gambling, prostitution, or commercial vice. To a significant extent, this seems to be the reality rather than merely a function of lax enforcement or underreporting in these categories. "Traditionally," crime on the reservations is preponderantly personal. One tribal judge, however, felt that this crime picture was slowly changing, with more people, especially among the younger generation, becoming involved in "white man's crimes" (against property). The Blackfeet statistics on burglary and larceny may reflect this new trend, as well as emphasize the jurisdictional/enforcement problems that would accompany such a trend. Though rare, prostitution, gambling, and commercial vice are not totally absent from the reservation scene either. Gambling, especially, is reported to be a popular activity among the Indians. Offenses like forgery, fraud, or embezzlement—"white-collar crimes"—are quite obviously not engaged in by the masses of reservation residents. On the other hand, numerous complaints of fraud and embezzlement of tribal funds and property are leveled against tribal government officials. Several informants—Indian and non-Indian—asserted that such fraudulent activity was a "way of life" for reservation officials. It may be that the Blackfeet statistics showing a measure of enforcement activity in this area of offenses indicate that "something is being done" about this problem. That the lack of such activity on Standing Rock indicates an absence of the problem is *not* likely to be an accurate assumption.

Narcotics offenses are portrayed as very infrequent in the

reservation statistics. This, again, appears to be a situation that is changing and one where law-enforcement activity and reporting have not yet caught up with reality. Informants, including tribal judges from three reservations, seemed to feel that the narcotics problem was becoming serious, if it was not already. Primarily young people were involved, and marijuana use and "glue sniffing" were said to be the common activities. On the Navajo Reservation, the traditional peyote drug is still used by people from a cross-section of generations. The law-enforcement stance toward peyote use did not become clear.[48]

To try to make reservation versus nonreservation comparisons among subtotals or individual crime categories is even more hazardous than comparing the total crimes. One misses the compensation for definitional inconsistencies which occurs in related categories of cases and which gives a measure of validity to the total figures. In looking at drunkenness arrests *only,* for example, one remains ignorant of the trade-off that often occurs between that category and related ones such as disorderly conduct, not to mention more remotely connected possibilities like vagrancy, vandalism, and assault. This only serves to exacerbate the already-staggering comparison difficulties caused by different enforcement patterns and recording systems between reservation and nonreservation societies, among reservations, and within any one system over time. With these misgivings in mind, I present in table 5 below comparative figures on three crime categories, heavily related to alcohol abuse, which appear to be especially serious problems on the reservations.

In addition to the total volume of crime and disputes on reservations and its breakdown into individual classes of cases, the issues of what actually is handled in the tribal courts (jurisdiction and its impact) and the dispositional patterns must also be addressed.

For the Standing Rock and Blackfeet reservations, the crime statistics include "major crimes" coming under federal jurisdiction. The statistics themselves, as officially produced and distri-

---

48. See Native American Church v. Navajo Tribal Council, 272 F.2d 131 (10th Cir. 1959), to the effect that some 15-20 years ago the Navajo tribal government tried to ban peyote use.

buted, indicate a cutoff point between auto theft and arson, with everything above the line labeled "Part I Offenses"; and everything below, "Part II." The implication that Part I offenses are all federal crimes and that the remainder are all within the

TABLE 5   Arrest Rate for Selected Offenses, per 100,000

	Rate per 100,000			
	United States (1974)	Standing Rock (1971, 1972)[a]	Blackfeet (1973)	Navajo (1974)
Driving while intoxicated . .	459.8	1,090.1	1,750.0	1,938.3
Drunkenness	680.1	13,300.0	1,450.0	8,366.7[b]
Disorderly conduct	406.0	4,872.7	24,300.0	

[a]Totals for the years 1971 and 1972 were added together and then divided by 2 to reduce the trade-off effect of atypical enforcement-reporting practices in 1971.

[b]This figure represents the rate for "offenses against the public peace" on the Navajo Reservation, a category roughly equivalent to drunkenness and disorderly conduct on the other reservations.

confines of tribal jurisdiction is, however, inaccurate. Arson is one of the enumerated major federal crimes and thus at least technically under federal jurisdiction. On the other hand, the assault cases listed in Part I include aggravated as well as less serious assaults—the latter being within tribal jurisdiction. Thus, it is not precisely clear what goes in the tribal court and what does not. The numbers in these jurisdictionally equivocal categories are comparatively small, however; on the Blackfeet Reservation, where they approach quantitative significance, it is mainly at the "reported or known to the police" level, with enforcement ("cleared by arrests") remaining low for a variety of reasons speculated about earlier.

The Navajo, Fort Totten, and Uintah and Ouray figures are strictly tribal court caseload statistics. Interviews with the Navajo chief justice, the tribal chief of police, and a federal prosecutor located in Albuquerque (characteristically far—some 150 miles—from the reservation) yielded a rough picture of about 700 major crimes committed annually on the Navajo Reservation. Less than 10 percent of these, however, resulted in prosecution, with the remainder reportedly sent back for tribal handling or dropped altogether—the latter two eventualities being roughly equivalent. Lack of interest and cooperation on the part of both federal and tribal officials as well as of witnesses and juries—caused by geographical and cultural distance—

and lack of manpower (again both tribal and federal) were cited
as being responsible for this pattern of little or no enforcement.
Interviews on other reservations revealed law enforcement with
respect to major crimes to be equally inadequate.

Only for the Navajo courts was it possible to obtain civil case
statistics of some detail and reliability. About 40 percent of the
Navajo civil caseload consisted of domestic relations problems,
including divorce, separation, adoption, custody, and guardian-
ship. Two other major categories of civil cases were contract/
commercial problems and the usual unspecified "other" classifi-
cation. The remainder of the civil actions were a smattering of
probate/trust, landlord/tenant, and land/grazing/fencing cases
and even an isolated mental health commitment. Observation
indicated that a good percentage of the civil court cases were
consensual in nature—formalizations of agreements already
arrived at informally.

That only 5 percent of the total tribal caseload are civil cases
may appear to indicate an "underuse" of the tribal court for
civil matters. One would not want to argue that the civil case
volume should be anywhere near the enormous criminal volume.
Nor is there any basis for wanting to see the Navajo approach
the litigiousness of the larger society. Still, noncriminal problems
and disputes do not appear to be scarce on the reservation: in
fact the opposite impression is strong with regard both to disputes among Indians and to problems between Indians and
whites (the charge that white merchants "rip off" Indian con-
sumers is one of the most common complaints). Thus, the 1,500
civil caseload may well be smaller than is appropriate and
healthy in reservation society.[49] This conclusion is supported by
testimony—specifically from a former tribal judge (an Indian)
and a white "visiting" tribal judge—to the effect that very low
civil use of the tribal courts is a pattern typical of most, if not

---

[49] For example, in 1975-76 the civil caseload in Livingston County, Ill.—a rural
county that is average in a number of demographic and economic respects (40,690
total population; $9,611 median family income)—almost equaled the criminal caseload
(excluding traffic cases). During that year there were 1,174 criminal cases (121
juvenile, 210 felony, and 843 misdemeanor) versus 1,042 civil matters (which is
equivalent to a rate per 100,000 population of 2,885 criminal cases and 2,561 civil
cases). By contrast the Navajo rates per 100,000 are 24,075 criminal and 1,253 civil
cases.

all, reservations. It has been suggested that considerable, and presumably adequate, dispute resolution still occurs through informal traditional (noncourt) channels. But the idea that these informal methods fill the vacuum of court "underuse" does not seem very plausible, especially for those reservations outside the exceptionally "traditional" ones in the Southwest. The slack is not taken up by the state courts either. If they are reluctant to resort to the *tribal* courts for civil matters, the Indians are equally reluctant to go to the state courts. The situation is not helped by the fact that the state courts are likely to be less than hospitable to civil claims made by reservation Indians against fellow Indian residents on reservations that do have operating tribal courts. In fact, absent a formal cession of jurisdiction by the tribal court and a formal assumption of it by the state, the situation seems to be that the state has no legal jurisdiction.[50]

How the tribal courts disposed of their criminal caseloads was presented in short tables immediately following the volume statistics for each of the reservations where this information was available. In table 6 below, this information is combined and compared with dispositional patterns for criminal cases in the United States.[51]

TABLE 6   Dispositional Patterns for Criminal Cases

	United States (1974)	Standing Rock (1972)	Blackfeet (1973)	Navajo (1974)[a]
Total no. charged	1,676,919[b]	1,626	3,319	10,975
Total no. guilty	63.3%	79.8%	62.7%	89.4%
Acquitted or dismissed . . .	18.4%	4.1%	17.2%	5.3%
Referred to juvenile court .	18.3%	13.8%	19.9%	----

[a]Based on the January-June 1975 sample. For a possible explanation of the disparity in totals, see reference on page 000 in text.

[b]The Uniform Crime Report here takes a sample of cases from 2,400 cities with a total population of 41,773,000.

50. See State ex rel. Adoption of Firecrow v. District Court, 536 P.2d 190 (1975); Fisher v. District Court, 424 U.S. 382 (1976).

51. Other possible comparisons have been suggested on the theory that these come closer to replicating the situations or caseloads with which the tribal courts are confronted. For example, comparison with the Municipal Court of Los Angeles has been pressed because a previous study makes statistics from that court and analysis of them available. James G. Holbrook, A Survey of Metropolitan Trial Courts—Los Angeles Area (Los Angeles: University of Southern California, 1956), especially at 315-18. The Los Angeles study shows an extremely high rate of pretrial dispositions in minor

The tribal court dispositional statistics show the conviction rates as well as the conviction totals to be quite high. Given also the very high incidence of criminal charges and arrests, one begins to perceive a hint of serious problems with tribal justice. In the reservation settings, how necessary is it to process such huge numbers? What good does it do? Is any person or agency exercising reasonable discretion about when and when not to involve the courts and criminal processes? I suggest that the answers are no. In much of the rest of this report I will be concerned with presenting details to substantiate this assessment. For the moment, it suffices to point out that a system that annually "convicts" numbers equivalent to 25-35 percent of its *total* population is perforce suspect.

OVERCRIMINALIZATION AND SUMMARY JUSTICE

In this section, while not moving away from numbers altogether, I present more qualitative, observational material and examine court records containing more substantive detail in an effort to portray the essence of tribal justice.

---

criminal matters (98 percent), but it is doubtful that that statistic can be compared with the tribal court situation. First, a pretrial disposition includes the possibility of dismissal; it is not equivalent to a guilty plea or a finding of guilty. More significantly, 79 percent of the "dispositions" were simple bail forfeitures—itself an indication of the lack of comparability with the tribal court situation (the nature of the offense, the status of the offender), where the offender is typically arraigned in person before the court, often via the reservation jail where he has spent, at minimum, one night. A brief separate discussion of "intoxication" cases in the Los Angeles courts yields the estimate that "approximately 90 percent of the persons charged with drunkenness pleaded guilty or were ultimately convicted" (*id.* at 317). The descriptive material indicates, however, that whatever the similarity of the numbers, the way guilty pleas or "convictions" are obtained in Los Angeles appears to be quite different from the way they are obtained on the reservations (more will be said on that subject later). In any case, it is difficult to see how a great deal of comfort can be derived from demonstrating that tribal courts duplicate some of the deficiencies of the worst of urban justice, particularly since the "excuses" of overwhelming volume and impersonality do not hold in the reservation setting.

A possibly more promising comparison is with a non-Indian rural county. The flaw in that is that the social, economic, and "crime" situations are very different. The crime picture on the reservations is to some extent a function of how the law-enforcement system chooses to operate; but quite obviously it is also more than that. There are also "real" differences. The following table shows the conviction rates for Livingston County, Ill. (see demographic, economic, and court data, *supra* note 49):

All crimes	66%
Felonies	70%
Misdemeanors (excluding traffic)	65%

Arraignments

Anyone who walks into a reservation courtroom on a typical weekday morning between about 9:30 and 10:30 is likely to find "arraignment" proceedings in progress. Involved may be 5, 10, 15, or, on the large reservations, up to 20 defendants. Perhaps one-third of these will be older men, chronic alcoholics, physically and psychologically ravaged by the condition, whose "offense" is public drunkenness, or, on reservations where there is an awareness that the criminal charge of public drunkenness may be constitutionally suspect, some legal refinement of that charge. Usually, the rest of the cases will also involve alcohol but can be distinguished on the facts that the accused are not chronic drinkers or that a separate concomitant offense is involved, such as assault and battery, vandalism, driving while intoxicated, or something along the line of disturbing the peace. One will be struck by the depressing overall scene: the majority of the accused appear to be so battered, bodily and spirtually, that one will question whether life, let alone the court proceeding in which they are involved, holds much meaning for them. Perhaps the night spent in the reservation jail, together with the aftereffects of the events preceding their arrest, make the appearance worse than "reality."

The tribal judges confronted with this setting usually make an attempt to communicate to the accused something relative to their rights at trial. Prompted at least in part, one suspects, by recent congressional concern about Indians' civil rights[52] these efforts by tribal judges take many forms, the impact of which on the whole appears to be negligible. That is to say, very few accused avail themselves of these rights, and those few who do appear to be motivated by considerations other than, or at least in addition to, the judge's communication[53] Some of the judges

---

52. E.g., the Senate Judiciary Committee hearings and their outgrowth, the Indian Civil Rights Act of 1968. 25 U.S.C. secs. 1302-3 (1975 Supp.).

53. Observations showed that the level of the defendant's awareness and his social standing, often coupled with the reality of his being represented by an expert, determined whether or not he entered a guilty plea. That is to say, on each reservation at least a small group of "well-connected" Indians knew how to "beat" the tribal court system, while the masses submitted to summary justice through guilty pleas made without advice or consideration of consequences or alternatives.

treat the rights issue as a bothersome but necessary formality and give it a short-shrift treatment not unlike police treatment of the "*Miranda* warning." Other tribal judges, however, are more conscientious about it and try to explain in layman's language the options of the accused, sometimes going as far as to look for nods of comprehension from them. Even under these circumstances, however, the impression is that most of the accused remain oblivious to the entire exercise. The chief judge on the Uintah and Ouray Reservation—possibly for the observer's benefit—got involved in such a lengthy explanation of "civil rights" that several of the accused fell asleep, the court reporter stopped taking notes, and the judge himself closed his eyes and lapsed into long pauses.

In the better-organized tribal courts (such as the Navajo court) arraignments are clearly separated from determinations on the merits; but in courts of less organizational efficacy, the two are sometimes confused. For example, during the fieldwork in the summer of 1974 on the Standing Rock Reservation, errors of this type occurred several times in the course of only a few days. When questioned on this point, the Standing Rock chief judge indicated that he knew his associates were falling into this error but that he had been unable to devise a way to put a stop to it.

Guilty Pleas

In a typical tribal court case (a pattern some tribal court judges see movement away from), the defendant immediately pleads guilty (at arraignment, without having received benefit of counsel, consultation, inquiry into the facts, consideration of alternatives, or bargaining) and is immediately sentenced (usually to serve a short jail term and/or to pay a fine). This occurs despite the fact that the complaint (as written and read) and the supporting affidavits (if present at all) often provide no details upon which the judge might base a reasoned decision, and sometimes fail altogether to state a crime or to provide grounds justifying the initial arrest.

Officially recorded and reported guilty plea rates are difficult to come by. In the Navajo courts for the first half of 1975, the guilty plea rate was about 85 percent. On other reservations, estimates by the court officials backed up by observations in the courts indicate that guilty plea rates are at least as high. Putting the reservation guilty plea phenomenon in a meaningful context is not a simple matter. It is well known of course that the guilty plea is a commonly used device in the state and federal courts as well; in felony cases, the rate has been around 60 percent in the recent years, with a general downward trend from the peak rate of a couple of decades ago.[54] There is a tremendous amount of variation, however, from jurisdiction to jurisdiction. Also, these are felony rates. One might expect the guilty plea rates for less serious cases to approximate the rates in the tribal courts. Figures from the Los Angeles Municipal Court, for example, seem to bear this out.[55] On the other hand, in rural areas the rates are likely to be lower.[56]

But the numbers do not mean a great deal. More significant than the quantitative comparison is a qualitative one. In state and federal courts, the guilty plea in felony cases—whatever its desirability or justifiability—is typically the product of deliberation, negotiation, and bargaining between counsel for the defense and the prosecution. Even in petty misdemeanors, defendants usually receive at least the formality of professional assistance, and at least some deliberation takes place before guilty pleas are entered and accepted.[57] By contrast, the pleas in the tribal courts are typically, if not invariably, untouched by such considerations. Finally, high guilty plea rates have been attacked as being a necessary evil at best and undesirable no matter what conditions foster them.[58]

---

54. See Michael O. Finkelstein, A Statistical Analysis of Guilty Plea Practices in the Federal Courts, 89 Harv. L. Rev. 293 (1975). For state figures, see 1 Lee Silverstein, Defense of the Poor in Criminal Cases in American State Courts: The National Report 92-93 (Chicago: American Bar Foundation, 1965); also Donald M. McIntyre & David Lippman, Prosecutors and Early Disposition of Felony Cases, 56 A.B.A.J. 1154, 1156 (1970), reprinted as ABF Research Contribution No. 2, 1971.

55. See Holbrook, supra note 51, at 315-18.

56. In Livingston County, Ill., the guilty-plea rate in misdemeanors (excluding traffic cases) was, at only 40 percent, significantly (20 percent) lower than the rate in felony cases (60 percent). The Livingston County figures may reflect the possibility that high guilty-plea rates are an urban response to massive misdemeanor caseloads and that there is less need for, and resort to, the plea in less crowded rural courts.

57. Holbrook, supra note 51, at 317-18. In urban courts, public defenders, groups of volunteer private lawyers, student "lawyers," and other such organizations provide service at the early stages of the criminal process. For the situation in rural courts, see the material at 126-42.

58. See Finkelstein, supra note 54, at 293, citing The President's Commission on Law Enforcement and the Administration of Justice, Task Force Report: The Courts 9 (1967).

With reference to the tribal courts, observers of and participants in the system (i.e., some of the tribal judges themselves) often contend that pleading guilty is a traditional Indian response to being accused and placed before a court. And, in the abstract, it is certainly not an inappropriate response. Surely there is sense in having defendants—whether Indian or non-Indian, sophisticated or unsophisticated—admit guilt and forgo wasteful contest to charges that are appropriately brought and understood. The reality that undercuts this simple sense, however, is that often charges are not well understood or brought: not in the non-Indian system, where the law-enforcement agencies are inclined to bring "excessive" charges, or in tribal courts, where the problem lies not only in the possibility of excess but also in the fact that the legal and commonsense sufficiency of the complaints is often as poorly understood by tribal law-enforcement officials as it is by the Indian defendants. If it is tradition that motivates defendants in tribal courts to plead guilty, one might well wonder whether the tradition is appropriate in the contemporary tribal justice context and whether tribal judges should accommodate it. Also, to the extent that the tradition is still operative, one can expect the Indian Civil Rights Act specifically and the ever increasing acculturation generally to result in its gradual erosion. However, my impression is that the guilty-plea response is part of the different and deeper problem of apathy which pervades contemporary reservation life and institutions. If so, changes in guilty-plea rates in the tribal courts will be harder to come by.

One may also try to explain the high frequency of the quick, unpremeditated guilty plea by pointing to the fact that the tribal courts handle only technically nonserious matters. Like the "tradition" rationale, however, this is not a full or satisfactory explanation, mainly because the formal limit on tribal court authority does not mean that there are *in fact* no serious matters before the courts. What it *does* mean is that serious cases get a limited level of treatment, which is all the tribal courts are equipped to provide. In courts of limited jurisdiction, which lack the staff, training, experience, and dispositional facilities to "do justice" to complex matters, serious cases in effect get reduced to fit the limited powers and capacities available. To the extent applicable, this reality supports the suggestion that the no-contest response, the guilty plea, is "forced" on tribal court defendants, as opposed to being a product of volition or tradition.

Summary Dispositions

The dominant characteristic of and in fact the main problem with tribal justice is that it is summary *regardless* of the complexity of the cases or the predispositions of the litigants. Irrespective of the nature of the case, there is not enough development of the legal facts that call the courts into operation or enough analysis of the individual circumstances to justify the dispositions. Significantly, and not coincidentally, in more than five weeks of observation in the tribal courts, only six fully contested cases were encountered, four of which were handled by white visiting judges. The remainder of the court activities, which occupied almost all the open-court time, consisted of the routine of taking guilty pleas; the occasional setting of a trial date, more often than not for the white judge's next visit or some other sporadic eventuality; a small number of consensual civil decrees; and a few aborted trials (one or two quick dismissals on technical grounds and a couple of "arraignments" resulting in summary disposition "on the merits"). I will later deal with the real problems involved in those isolated matters that were not treated in summary fashion.

The trouble with this pattern of summary justice is that the reservation *people* are entitled to more than that. The tribal courts are *the* judicial forum on the reservations. For the vast majority of people, tribal justice is all they know.[59] The tribal courts have an impact on a broad array of daily occurrences on the reservations: what they handle, they handle with essentially final authority; what they do not handle equally affects people's expectations regarding justice. The option of resort to alternative judicial forums is not a practical one. Federal involvement in "major crimes" is at best an isolated and usually nondefinitive phenomenon. State courts, doubtful of their authority, are reluctant to take on reservation problems from reservations with

---

59. For non-Indians, too, the typical experience is with the lower courts, but their option of appeal is more realistic.

tribal courts, a reluctance matched only by that of the reservation officials and people to bring their problems to state courts. Appeal from the tribal courts to the federal courts in individual cases (as opposed to tribal matters) is so rare as to be insignificant in the total flow of cases. Even appeal within the tribal system is of little practical value because of the insufficient differentiation between appellate and trial functions and personnel.

Complexity of Problems

By the same token, the reservation *problems* deserve more than summary justice. First, although there are a large number of arrests, the caseload in general does not *necessitate* mass, summary processing in the form of guilty pleas and the like. Nor is mass processing a *good* way to deal with numerous, recurring matters, even those of the innocuous variety. Second, many reservation problems are (deceptively, perhaps) complex and serious. The high volume of "crime" on the reservations is in itself serious: it indicates a degree of breakdown in the social processes and institutions of social control, regardless of whether individual behavior is actually serious by "objective" standards, or only thought to be so and treated as such by tribal police. Furthermore, a proportion of the "nonserious" cases involve significant legal principles that ought not be given short-shrift treatment simply on the grounds that the ultimate penalty is only six months in jail (as if that were nothing). Beyond that, criminal activity—as elsewhere, but especially on the reservations—is highly related to alcohol abuse, which suggests serious and complicating social and economic components: driving while intoxicated is a deadly habit that mandates more than the futile and repetitive routine of guilty plea and fine or jail; serious beatings and assaults (sometimes involving weapons or threats with weapons) and disturbances and harassments, often intrafamily ones, are other major alcohol-related problems; the same holds for problems like parental neglect of children and nonsupport; the fact that juveniles are so frequently involved in criminal offenses, with high rates of recidivism for both juveniles and adults, adds a special dimension of seriousness. On the civil side, long-standing and festering disputes over land use and ownership are among the more intricate legal and social problems: probate law, grazing and water-rights laws, and leasing rules provide the legal framework, while underneath may be complicating historical and social considerations such as traditional Indian notions of ownership and agreement; the federal trust role; state and other non-Indian individual claims; and so forth. In addition, there are difficult problems involving housing conditions, housing authorities, financing of sales or leases, bankruptcies, child custody, welfare rights, and defective products and the whole host of problems faced by persons of poor or moderate income. A satisfactory system cannot afford to dispose of this caseload with treatment that uniformly ranges from summary to nul, doled out by untrained "magistrates." No one would stand for this in the larger society. Why should it be good enough for the reservations?

Unwarranted Processing

The other side of the coin of simplistic and routinized handling of serious problems is the equally routine and indiscriminate criminal processing of genuinely nonserious (noncriminal?) matters. As can be inferred from the high arrest, charging, and conviction rates in the drunkenness and disorderly conduct type of offenses in particular (and as later details will confirm), the police and prosecution engage in little or no rational screening; and because of the absence of facts and their own limited perceptions about their role in getting the facts the tribal judges make dispositional decisions in a vacuum. Thus, it becomes easy for a basically law-abiding Indian who is found drunk one night and arrested while tribal police are breaking up a general disturbance to receive the same treatment as a repeat driving-while-intoxicated offender. Or, similarly, an Indian involved in an isolated marital transgression may be dealt with as harshly as, or more severely than, a genuinely and chronically criminal type. Official records of court dispositions on the Uintah and Ouray Reservation seem to confirm that such results are common. In addition, a small random sample of crime records from the Navajo Reservation gives an indication of the negative effect of the tribal court process on the individual and suggests that this routinized, overcriminalized approach to law and order is futile.

Table 7 catalogues the crimes and court dispositions drawn from 4 random pages of a 27-page report for the year 1969. (We were unable to obtain more recent records of this kind.) The proper names of the individuals have been replaced by numbers, and each case is given a different number even though the same defendant may be involved in several cases.

TABLE 7   Tribal Court Disposition on the Uintah and Ouray Reservation, 1969

Case No. and Charge	Disposition
1. Disorderly conduct	15 days in jail
2. Disorderly conduct	15 days in jail
3. Disorderly conduct	15 days in jail
4. Escape	15 days in jail
5. Disorderly conduct	6 months' probation
6. Disorderly conduct	$10 court fine
7. Disorderly conduct	Dismissed
8. Disorderly conduct	30 days' probation, due to ill health
9. Disorderly conduct	15 days in jail
10. Disorderly conduct	30 days in jail, released to go to school
11. Violation of approved tribal ordinance	1st charge, $30
&	
Failure to support dependent persons	2d charge, 3 months in jail
12. Assault & battery	6 months in jail, suspended, placed on probation
13. Disorderly conduct	Presentenced for evaluation
14. Disorderly conduct	Dismissed
15. Abduction	2-24-69, 6 months' probation
16. Disorderly conduct	$30
&	
Assault & battery	6 months in jail
17. Disorderly conduct	30 days' probation
18. Disorderly conduct	30 days' probation
19. Disorderly conduct	$10 or 10 days in jail
20. Disorderly conduct	$10 or 10 days in jail
21. Disorderly conduct	Dismissed
22. Disorderly conduct	Dismissed
23. Disorderly conduct	Presentence evaluation
24. Disorderly conduct	30 days in jail
25. Disorderly conduct	30 days in jail
26. Escape	6 months in jail
27. Disorderly conduct	10 days in jail
28. Disorderly conduct	30 days in jail
29. Disorderly conduct	Postponed trial
30. Disorderly conduct	25 days in jail or $25
31. Driving under the influence of alcohol	100 days in jail
32. Driving under the influence of alcohol	$100 fine
33. Driving under the influence of alcohol	$100 or 100 days
34. Escape	Cash bond $60
35. Violation of approved tribal ordinance	$30 and 30 days in jail

TABLE 7—continued

Case No. and Charge	Disposition
36. Disorderly conduct	Case dismissed
37. Disorderly conduct & Aiding an escape	30 days in jail
38. Driving under the influence of alcohol	$5 fine
39. Disorderly conduct	Presentenced to evaluation. Sentenced to 30 days in jail, suspended; placed on 60 days' probation on 2 counts with the Ute Indian Tribal Alcoholism Program
40. Disorderly conduct	30 days in jail, suspended; placed with Ute Indian Tribal Alcoholism Program
41. No signal or brake lights	Case dismissed
42. Disorderly conduct	Cash bond $60
43. Driving under the influence of intoxicants	$100 or 100 days in jail
44. No tail lights	$15 or 15 days in jail
45. Disorderly conduct	$25 or 15 days in jail
46. Property damage	Suspended sentence
47. Disorderly conduct	$10 or 10 days in jail
48. Driving under the influence of intoxicants	$125 or 125 days in jail
49. No driver's license	$5
50. No driver's license	$5
51. No driver's license	$5, will pay on December 20
52. Illicit cohabitation	30 days in jail or get married
53. Illicit cohabitation	30 days in jail
54. Illicit cohabitation	30 days in jail
55. Illicit cohabitation	30 days in jail
56. Disorderly conduct	20 days in jail
57. Disorderly conduct	15 days in jail
58. Illicit cohabitation	30 days in jail
59. Illicit cohabitation	30 days in jail
60. Disorderly conduct	30 days in jail
61. Illicit cohabitation	30 days in jail
62. Reckless driving	$25 or 25 days in jail
63. Disorderly conduct	10 days in jail
64. Illicit cohabitation	Dismissed
65. Illicit cohabitation	30 days in jail
66. Illicit cohabitation	20 days in jail
67. Disorderly conduct	$15 or 15 days in jail
68. Illicit cohabitation	30 days in jail
69. Disorderly conduct	$15 or 15 days in jail
70. Disorderly conduct	$15 or 15 days in jail
71. Disorderly conduct	$15 or 15 days in jail
72. Illicit cohabitation	30 days in jail
73. Disorderly conduct	$10 or 10 days in jail
74. Disorderly conduct	5 days in jail
75. Disorderly conduct	$20 or 20 days in jail
76. Disorderly conduct	$30 or 15 days in jail
77. Violation of approved tribal ordinance	$10 or 10 days in jail
78. Violation of approved tribal ordinance	$10 and 10 days in jail
79. Violation of approved tribal ordinance	$10 and 10 days in jail

TABLE 7—continued

Case No. and Charge	Disposition
80. Violation of approved tribal ordinance	$10 and 10 days in jail
81. Disorderly conduct	Case dismissed
82. Disorderly conduct	Case dismissed
83. Disorderly conduct	20 days in jail
84. Disorderly conduct	20 days in jail
85. Disorderly conduct	30 days in jail, suspended; placed on probation to alcohol center
86. Disorderly conduct	5 days in jail
87. Disorderly conduct	25 days in jail
88. Resisting lawful arrest	15 days in jail

In these court-disposition records, as with the arrest data presented earlier, the high proportion of disorderly conduct charges stands out. The outcomes vary, but it can be seen that many of them are pretty stiff jail sentences. Another outstanding feature is the high number of illicit-cohabitation cases. Thirty days in jail appears to be the uniform disposition. Both as compared with dispositions in other matters and in terms of prevailing reservation mores, these seem like harsh and moralistic sentences. Although a separate sociological study would be needed to substantiate this, the informants who spoke on the issue indicated that marital transgressions of the type covered by the illicit-cohabitation charge were commonly and conspicuously engaged in on the reservations. As with the whole of "tribal law," the illicit-cohabitation offense is in the codes because white officials either put it there or put it in the models upon which the codes are based. That it has remained there to the present day and continues to be enforced is a different matter. On the Sioux and Blackfeet reservations, illicit cohabitation appeared to be less significant in the law-enforcement schemes. On the Navajo Reservation, illicit cohabitation was one of the charges in the major case observed in the tribal court; the overall incidence of the offense and its enforcement, however, lay buried in the records under the general headings of "offenses against the family and children" and "sexual misconduct."

Another notable aspect of the Uintah and Ouray dispositions is the prevalence of the fine or jail alternative. This remains a favorite sentence on all reservations, despite the fact that the constitutionality of this alternative is now suspect in off-reservation courts and perforce in the tribal courts as well.[60] The poorer Indians, of course, stand to lose in the application of a jail or fine alternative, as they do in the bail practices. Release on one's own recognizance is a barely known concept in tribal law enforcement, and its application is even less evident. No matter how innocuous the offense, the tribal judges tend to set bail at a stiff level ($60 minimum on the Uintah and Ouray Reservation) because they think the defendants would not show up otherwise. This situation, combined with high arrest and charging rates, results in a good portion of the reservation residents—but especially the poorer ones—finding themselves in and out of jail with considerable regularity. An indication to that effect is found in six criminal records picked at random from the Navajo files (see table 8).

TABLE 8   Criminal Records of Six Navajo Defendants

Charge	Disposition
Defendant A:	
1967 . . . Reckless driving	Suspended sentence
1967 . . . Drunk driving	$30 fine or 15 days
1967 . . . Liquor violation	$15 fine or 10 days
1964 . . . Disorderly conduct	$14 fine or 5 days
1963 . . . Reckless & drunk driving	$10 fine or 5 days
1963 . . . Driving without license	Dismissed (presented license)
1963 . . . Reckless driving	$10 fine or 10 days
1962 . . . Disorderly conduct	$10 fine or 10 days
1959 . . . Disorderly conduct	$10 fine or 10 days
1959 . . . Disorderly conduct	$10 fine or 10 days
Defendant B:	
1973 . . . Speeding	$30 fine or 15 days
1973 . . . Driving without license	$20 fine or 10 days
1973 . . . Drunk driving	45 days (no fine alternative, but placed on probation after serving 7 days)
1972 . . . Failure to stop at sign	$8 fine or 4 days
Defendant C:	
1975 . . . Disorderly conduct	Dismissed (no reason given)
1975 . . . Disorderly conduct	$25 or 10 days
1974 . . . Disorderly conduct	$20 or 10 days
1974 . . . Disorderly conduct	$10 or 5 days
1973 . . . Disorderly conduct	$5 or 5 days
1972 . . . Liquor violation	$20 or 20 days
1972 . . . Disorderly conduct	$22 or 22 days
1970 . . . Driving vehicle without brakes	$10 or 10 days
1969 . . . Disorderly conduct	$22 or 22 days
1967 . . . Disorderly conduct	$15 or 15 days
1964 . . . Liquor violation	$30 or 30 days

60. See Tate v. Short, 401 U.S. 395 (1974).

TABLE 8—continued

	Charge	Disposition
Defendant D:		
1972 . . .	Drunk driving	Dismissed (no prosecution)
1972 . . .	Liquor violation	$10 or 5 days
1969 . . .	Reckless & drunk driving	Reckless charge dismissed; drunk driving conviction, $100 fine (paid) or 25 days (served 7 days)
1969 . . .	Liquor violation	60 day probation
1967 . . .	Disorderly conduct	$20 or 7 days
1967 . . .	Vehicle with faulty tail lights	Dismissed (has valid license)
1966 . . .	Reckless driving	15 days (no fine alternative)
Defendant E:		
1972 . . .	Resisting arrest	$20 or 10 days (served 3 days)
1972 . . .	Liquor violation	$20 or 10 days (served 3 days)
1972 . . .	Drunk driving	30 days' probation
1968 . . .	Reckless driving	$100 or 25 days (served 25 days)
1967 . . .	Disorderly conduct	$20 or 10 days
1965 . . .	Disorderly conduct	$45 or 30 days (served 4 days)
1964 . . .	Disorderly conduct	15 days' probation
1963 . . .	Nonsupport	Dismissed on motion of complaining witness
1961 . . .	Disorderly conduct	Dismissed
1961 . . .	Liquor violation	Dismissed (after spending over 36 hours in jail prior to trial)
Defendant F:		
1971 . . .	No passing zone, no license	Dismissed

One would not want to base a broad general conclusion on such a limited sample, but it presents a discouraging picture. Four of the six defendants have long records of recurring identical violations. The dispositions have obviously not been a deterrent. In addition, they are difficult to rationalize. As with the Uintah and Ouray dispositions, whether an individual is fined or jailed or gets a choice appears to be largely unrelated to the recorded charge. One could argue, perhaps, that the relation is to be found in circumstances that are not in the record. But given the nature of the tribal court process, this is unlikely. In the typical case, the judge would have no facts other than the police complaint or charge and no indications of the defendant's past or present circumstances or behavior. Furthermore, the immediate guilty plea, the pattern in the vast majority of cases, precludes the subsequent development of these facts. Once in a while the charge may be accompanied by a supporting affidavit from the police which elaborates beyond the mere statement of the "crime." But supporting affidavits usually leave a good deal to be desired. Two examples follow:

Subject was observed passed out along with subjects, lying down in a very disorderly condition, when checked him, had strong odor of alcohol smelled from his breath also unable to walk without staggering when told to walk, therefore was in custody.

That the above name defendant was found on the road north of [Town X] turn-off. That he was with a party namely [individuals A, B, and C]. There was a accident and the traffic was block for two miles. That these party drove up in a 64 dodge pickup and try to get through the traffic. So for this reason the Police Investigate and one beer and one part wine were conforcated.

These examples are not to make fun but to illustrate that a guilty plea and a disposition based on this kind of information, which is *more* than is usually available, pose as many problems as the cases that come unencumbered with such detail.

Finally, some of the Navajo dispositions contained a notation to the effect that part of the jail sentence had been served. The Navajo judges stated that this conformed to a common occurrence: a defendant who was unable to pay the fine would begin serving the jail-term alternative until a friend or relative came up with the money. While not entirely clear, the information seemed to indicate that this could also happen when only a jail sentence was involved. Even in that case, it would be possible for a friend or relative to make a plea on behalf of the jailed defendant, based on his indispensability around the house or at work, and get him released by paying off the remaining jail term at a rate of $2.00 per day. If the record contained no notation of time served, the defendant had either served the full jail term or paid the full fine forthwith.

There are relatively few civil cases in the tribal courts, and civil records are largely unavailable. On the Navajo Reservation, however, where it was possible to examine civil case records, the records were not susceptible of much meaningful interpretation. One got the impression—perhaps as much from observations and interviews as from the records themselves—that the process of civil litigation lacked balance. Typically, the record showed that only one of the parties was represented and that the outcome favored that party. But in order to determine more accurately what takes place in civil cases, one would have to rely more on direct observation. The sections ahead will deal with observations of both civil and criminal complaints. So as to convey the flavor of the tribal court process, I will present my observations

in more or less anecdotal fashion. The scene on three reservations is presented in detail in the text. Discussion of the remaining two is in the appendix, which also contains the comparative
observations on the state courts. Some theory and analysis will
follow the descriptive section.

THE STANDING ROCK SYSTEM

The Standing Rock Sioux Indian Reservation, which straddles
the North and South Dakota border on the west bank of the
Missouri River, is located on basically empty and barren land,
almost treeless, cold in winter and often hot in the summer.
Sloping down to the river from the flat to slightly rolling plains
of the Dakotas, much of the reservation land area is marked by
low buttes and hills—remnants of an earlier unbroken plateau
and "elevations" only in relation to the basic (and more recent)
erosive and depressive character of the landscape. The river bot-
tom land was once (not so long ago) forested and filled with
game, but much of it has been inundated since the construction
of the Oahe Dam (begun in 1948 and completed in 1963); now
about all that is left are small forests of dead and leafless trees
sticking out of the river-reservoir waters. Sitting Bull's original
burial site, too, is now under water, a grimly symbolic casualty
of technological progress.
    Until recently, the southern boundaries of the reservation
were viewed as ending at the North-South Dakota border, and
most road maps still have it that way. But the "exterior" boundaries of the reservation have now been officially recognized as
extending well into South Dakota, about to Mobridge, a town
on the east bank of the Missouri some 30 miles south of the
North Dakota line.[61] The area included within these outer
boundaries contains much white-owned land, however, including
relatively "significant" towns such as McLaughlin and McIntosh
(population about 600 and 900, respectively), which are predominantly white. The North Dakota part of the reservation is

---

61. In fact, by today's boundaries, as much as two-thirds of the "reservation's"
total acreage is in South Dakota. About one-half the reservation population in both
South and North Dakota is non-Indian. Tribal court jurisdiction is not asserted over
the non-Indian population, and the notion that it ought to be in a situation of this
kind is difficult to take seriously.

more exclusively Indian, with the Indian town Fort Yates serving as the county seat of Sioux County, North Dakota, and as capital of the reservation. Transportation to and from the reservation is poor: only the white towns of Mobridge, McLaughlin, and McIntosh are accessible by a decent highway. Fort Yates can be reached only by going at least part of the way on narrow county roads; the nearest bridge across the Missouri is at Bismarck, more than 70 miles to the north, or at Mobridge, more than 50 miles south of Fort Yates.

The Indian population of the Standing Rock Reservation is somewhere between 4,500 and 6,000, depending on who defines and counts. There is not much work. Much of the ranching or farming that does take place on the reservation is done by whites who either own or lease the land.[62] Similarly, concerns such as grocery stores, gas stations, motels, and bars are often owned and operated by whites—though this is gradually changing in favor of greater Indian control and participation in these ventures. The majority of the Indians live in towns and settlements spread around the reservation, with about one-quarter of the total population residing at Fort Yates. Employment, such as there is in these towns, is often in federal government or tribal government positions; and, as noted before, there is much unemployment.

The main court is in Fort Yates, North Dakota, but a branch office operates out of McLaughlin, South Dakota. A large new trailer is being built on the outskirts of McLaughlin for the branch court and law-enforcement personnel who have temporary offices in the basement of the welfare building. The McLaughlin court staff consists of an associate judge and a clerk-secretary. In Fort Yates, there are two associate judges in addition to the chief judge, who handles trial (arraignment) work as well as administrative chores. A white lawyer from Lemmon, South Dakota—just outside the reservation boundaries—comes in periodically (one or two times a month at one time, but now less often) to conduct trials in important or complex cases. Originally, important or complex cases meant anything beyond arraignment, but the Indian judges are beginning

---

62. Recall the quotation from Price on land use, *supra* note 25.

to assume greater responsibility. The Fort Yates court also has a probation and a juvenile officer. Neither the judges nor their supporting personnel have had formal training for their jobs.[63] Representation for defendants or plaintiffs is occasionally provided by the one mixed-blood lay advocate who fills this function (without pay) on the reservation. There is no prosecutor for the Standing Rock tribal court.

The statistics concerning tribal justice on Standing Rock have been given in the previous section; here I wish to present descriptive material gathered in my fieldwork.

The chief judge of the Standing Rock tribal court has been in office less than a year,[64] and as a result is still feeling his way around. His own perception, which he volunteers immediately, but which in retrospect appears to be questionable in view of the range and severity of other difficulties, is that the main problem facing the court is its lack of independence from the tribal council. He illustrates this first by saying that "they select us; they pay us . . . ," as if no further elaboration were needed. When pressed for details, it comes out that council members telephone him frequently: "What about so and so?" or, "you've been setting bail too high." But even the most elaborate incident he reports remains vague: "The other day they called me up about these guys who were arrested—they needed them back to play in the band Saturday night [at some tribal function]." Other informants on the reservation—a friend of a council member, a former tribal judge, a local businessman—are more vehement in denouncing council interference as a major problem. But concrete instances and details that can be followed up and substantiated are hard to come by.

The chief judge's performance on the bench is halting and unsure. Off the bench, he makes no attempt to hide his lack of confidence in being able to handle the legal and administrative complexities of his job. He expresses despair at the problems of

---

63. There have been changes in this respect since the time the fieldwork was done. See *infra* note 64.
64. Since this writing, the chief judgeship has again turned over and is now filled by a younger man, an Indian professional lawyer (who is *not* a native of Standing Rock Reservation). This new information was accompanied by complaints that made it clear that the new judge was seen as an intruder.

keeping his associates in line and bringing some form and regularity to the proceedings of the court. He admits his disinclination to tangle with lawyers and juries, adding that, if at all possible, he leaves cases of any complexity for the white lawyer-judge. Substantive legal problems are complicated by uncertainties and changes in the law. The tribal court, for example, has momentarily stopped handling domestic relations cases, according to the judge, because of a change coming up in the state law on which, for lack of tribal code provisions, the Standing Rock court depends. The handling of juvenile offenders is at a standstill because the state no longer honors tribal court decrees of commitment to the state reform system. The local jail is currently the only alternative. The judge reports that similar difficulties have beset the court's attempt to deal with alcoholics. The tribal council, presumably in an effort to be in tune with the latest developments in law, has amended the tribal code so as to preclude judicial commitments to detoxification centers and hospitals. Henceforth, only medical commitments will be legal. Since there are no doctors on the reservation, the upshot is that the newly built "detox" center stands empty.[65]

The judge describes a case involving parental neglect which reveals a problem of a different order: The parents of three Indian boys who had been placed in a foster school but who were home for a temporary visit petitioned the tribal court to allow the boys to remain home for good. The director of the foster school opposed this petition. While making clear that all his sentiments were with the boys and their parents, the judge decided in favor of sending the boys back to the school because of his reluctance to second-guess the judgment of "educated professionals," as he put it, and of his uncertainty about the jurisdictional power of the tribal court.

In this case, the lack of confidence on the part of the judge worked to preclude the kind of "local," "Indian" problem resolution that one presumes is one of the main raisons d'être of the tribal court system.

---

65. The lack of practical wisdom in this move needs no elaboration. Even theoretically, it is dubious to leave such decisions *exclusively* in the hands of medical people. Nor does such a theory represent the latest trend, if that is to be viewed as a reason for adopting it.

Associate Judge A makes a more reassuring first impression, which, on reflection and on the basis of reports from other reservation informants, threatens to be somewhat illusory. His performance on three cases that I observed perhaps speaks for itself.

The first case concerns a 19-year-old Indian boy caught driving without a license. Appearing with his mother, who does half the talking for him, the youth generally looks and acts younger than his age. The response to the charge is that he just got out of the service and has not had time to get a license, or a job for that matter. The judge is very restrained; the proceedings resemble an informal conference much more than a court case. At the end, the judge imposes a fine of $10 plus $4 court costs, which is to be paid, as he states explicitly, when the defendant gets a job with the Youth Corps or when the mother gets her next welfare check.

Shortly after this traffic case, an Indian woman walks in to the office to complain that the (white) postal clerk in McLaughlin is withholding her welfare check. The judge's response is to have the court clerk immediately type out a tribal court decree ordering release of the check. No attempt is made to handle the complaint formally, or to discover whether or why the postal clerk has in fact withheld the check.

During the proceedings, two very drunk and ravaged-looking Indian men are lounging around just outside the judge's office. They take a swig from a bottle from time to time, being careful to do this when the judge is not looking. It turns out one of the men is the court clerk's husband. It is payday for court personnel, and apparently he is waiting to relieve his wife of her paycheck. The judge, who is well aware of what is transpiring, responds to the situation by having the clerk type up a formal looking "restraining order" against the husband. He explains that this is a preventive measure often used on the reservation (and on other reservations, as later observations will show) in that it threatens immediate arrest and punishment upon violation of the order—not to "bother" the wife in this particular case.

At first glance, these cases may appear to indicate a swift and informal dispensation of "justice." Some questions surface later: Is the extreme informality and leniency displayed in the traffic case good policy in an environment where, as the judge himself points out, the flouting of traffic regulations and uncontrolled and drunken driving are virtually a tradition? In the postal clerk case, does the issuance of a court order without factual or legal foundation serve any reasonable interest? As for the restraining order against the husband, what is its effectiveness or legality? One cynical answer, implied by one Indian tribal official, is that none of it makes any difference, because in effect Judge A is completely powerless and anyone who wants to ignore his orders does so. This picture of the judge's ineffectiveness is probably too pessimistic, just as the initial favorable impression was too optimistic.

The experience in the court while Associate Judge B is on the bench is, however, unequivocally negative. Scheduled are seven "arraignments" (at least that is what the judge announces), but it turns out that two cases reach the "merits." The court begins with the judge reading a statement concerning the trial rights of defendants. Then the complaints are examined. This is a very confusing process. After many hesitations and rereadings, the result is that three defendants plead guilty, two plead not guilty and have trial dates and bond set, and two cases reach the merits.

One of the guilty pleas is obtained under the following circumstances: The charge is assault and battery, and the judge asks the defendant (who is characteristically without witnesses or representation), "Last time you pleaded not guilty—do you *still* plead not guilty?" The defendant then pleads guilty.

In one of the "arraignments" reaching the merits, a young Indian woman who is accompanied by her mother is charged with driving without a license. There is no real plea; instead, speaking up from the spectator seats, the mother points out that the charge, if anything, is supposed to be driving without taillights. No police officer or other accusing witnesses are in court. Eventually a shouting match (some of it in the tribal language) develops between the mother and the judge, to which the judge puts an abrupt end by finding the defendant guilty and assessing a fine. The mother just smiles in contempt, gets out her wallet, and waves some bills at the judge. That is the end of the case.

During the afternoon session in Judge B's court, five Indian adolescents are facing a charge of contributing to the delinquency of a minor. Unlike the more typical downtrodden tribal court defendants, these are the relatively well-off, well-dressed children of BIA and tribal officials. They are quite vocal, arguing out loud with the judge from the spectator seats and clearly contemptuous of him. They manage to point out that the dates on the warrants are wrong, succeed in having the case dismissed, and walk out laughing. The disadvantaged alcoholic defendant may have no more respect for the court than these kids. By not showing his disrespect, however, and by standing mute or mumbling a guilty plea instead of exploiting his trial rights and technicalities, he becomes a statistic in the "convicted" category.

The case of the misdated warrants turns out to be no isolated instance. When queried about it later, the chief judge confides that whole stacks of warrants are simply "lost" by the police, court orders are not carried out, fines not paid, and summonses and subpoenas are simply ignored.[66]

Given the picture of the Indians as victims, it seems inappropriate to worry excessively about the whites who may be disadvantaged by the tribal court, troubling as the individual case may be. One such case involving a small-time white rancher who lives on Standing Rock Reservation illustrates general court problems: Before he begins the morning court session, Judge B is confronted outside the courtroom by a fiftyish white man; giving much emphasis to a piece of paper in his possession, the man tries to tell the judge about how two wealthy ranchers (one Indian, one half-Indian) are running their cattle across his land on the pretext that the land does not belong to him. The piece of paper is a handwritten tribal court "decree," authored by Judge B himself, which has relevance to the man's claim that the land is rightfully his. Precisely what the relevance is is difficult to say; the decree, in misspelled pseudolegalese, purports to grant the holder "authority" to sell. Judge B, who apparently doesn't know what to make of it anymore, lamely winds up by advising

---

66. Ordinary reservation residents to whom I spoke informally displayed much cynicism about the tribal justice process; the term "kangaroo court" cropped up regularly. What makes the situation worse is that, as in most tribal courts but especially in the Standing Rock court, the right to appeal tribal court decisions is not meaningful. The chief judge on Standing Rock, who plays the main appellate role, explicitly stated that he thought his job as an appeals judge was to "stand behind" and support his associate judges.

the man to go see the county attorney. The incident, apart from illustrating problems of legal competence and confidence, also gives rise to an impression that will become stronger—if never totally "provable"—through observations and interviews on other reservations: the powerless (whether Indian or white) cannot count on the tribal courts for protection against the caprices of the few who are wealthy and powerful on the reservations.

The performance of Associate Judge C of the Standing Rock court is not more encouraging. There are four arraignments one morning when he is on the bench. The first three accused plead guilty to a variety of drinking-related charges and are fined/sentenced forthwith. The fourth, a young Indian of about 20, is faced with a number of charges and complaints centering around the destruction of private property, read off with difficulty by the judge. He chooses to be "untraditional":

Judge: How do you plead?
Accused: Not guilty.
Judge: But they showed me the window [of the car]; it was completely broken; I saw it, it was completely gone.
Accused: I don't know. I didn't do it.
Judge: You'd been drinking, right . . .?
Accused: [Shrugs and mumbles something to the effect of "not guilty."]
Judge: I know I saw that window all broken.
Accused: [Same as previous response.]
Judge: The court finds you guilty and fines you $20 plus 20 days in jail.

The judge follows then with a long and heartfelt lecture about young peoples' drinking. His sincerity as well as his exasperation about what he sees happening on the reservation is obvious. But this is irrelevant. The reservation Indians regard him as senile at best; two informants complain that he is a harsh "letter-of-the-law S.O.B."

Professional lawyers do not represent litigants in the tribal court of Standing Rock Reservation. Everyone is essentially on his own, given that there is no prosecutor, lay or professional, and no lay legal aid or defender's office. There is one Indian lay advocate, with only a high school education, who takes an isolated case here and there. Though he tries hard, his performance is understandably uneven and inadequate. His own conception of his role in the tribal court process, as any objective assessment of it must also be, is ambivalent. Yet, a description of the cases in which he was observed in action reveals that he is not useless or inconsequential.

The first case involves four teen-age Indian girls who have allegedly smashed the car windows of the local (white) barber by pelting them with empty beer bottles at 2:00 one morning. The case is tried before the white lawyer-judge and an all-Indian jury. It is rare for Indian defendants to request juries,[67] though it appears that they have a paramount interest in doing so if the common assertion (from many sources) that Indian juries "never convict" is accurate.[68] After the complainant—in the absence of a prosecutor—relates his version of the incident, the lay defender gets a shot at him. He is very aggressive and asks numerous factual questions on the order of how many beer bottles were thrown; how could the complainant tell since it was 2 a.m. and dark; whether his car windows were intact before 2 a.m.; and so forth. Substantively they are not very incisive questions, and the complainant's case is not really damaged. They have a psychological impact, however. The young defendants' confidence is boosted; they smile at each other from time to time and seem impressed with the bits of legal jargon the advocate manages to slip in periodically. It is more difficult to assess the impact on the jury, which is composed of five old women and one old man. At least one is asleep; the others sit through the proceedings impassively. It may well be that they cannot hear most of what is taking place, since the courtroom radiator is making an awful racket. True to reputation—but not out of line with the facts as developed at trial—their verdict is not guilty.

---

67. The AILTP survey, *supra* note 31, reports that there were 10 jury trials in 1975. Relative to the numbers in other tribal courts, this is high.

68. There are no statistics to substantiate this, only the assessments of the people who are familiar with the tribal court system, that is, the judges, lawyers, and lay advocates. The assessment is plausible in view of the fact that the isolated defendant who has a full jury trial is also likely to have the help of a lay advocate, perhaps even a professional one. With no professional judge or prosecutor to check him, the defense advocate has comparatively little trouble creating doubts about the case against the defendant. Other factors that might contribute to juries failing to convict are: (a) antipathy toward tribal authority (represented here by the tribal justice system) on the part of a good portion of the reservation population; (b) fear of reprisals; (c) kinship between one or more members of the jury and the defendant.

In two other cases, the advocate's tactics and impact are more disruptive, and arguably less desirable. The cases are technically arraignments, but they go well beyond the usual quick guilty plea.

In one case, the 18-year-old daughter of an influential Indian resident of Standing Rock Reservation is charged with three counts growing out of a single incident of drinking and fighting. After some haggling between the advocate and the judge, during which the former *asks* the latter whether he has properly advised the defendant "of the Fifth Amendment" and gratuitously adds that defendants should not be allowed to waive rights because by waiving them they show they do not understand them, the proceedings really bog down on the issue of whether the defendant in the instant case has a right to a separate jury trial (on different dates) on each count. Apparently believing that a maximum disruption of the court process and the greatest consumption of court time will be of maximum benefit to the defendant, the advocate presses hard for separation. The judge, who simply does not know how to deal with this tactic, defers any decision until later.

In the next case, in which a 16-year-old Indian boy is charged with assault, the proceedings really get out of hand. The complainants are a boy, about the same age as the accused, and his mother. The advocate, representing the accused, and the complainant-mother have taken over the court and are yelling at each other while the judge only looks on with a pained and tired expression. At first, the gist of the dispute is over whether there has been any assault at all. The advocate ultimately concedes that there has, admitting that he "confused assault with battery." The fact is, however, that there is about as little basis for that arrest/charge as there is for battery.[69] From what can

---

69. The case illustrates what, as one local lawyer living just off the reservation described explicitly, is a general and fundamental problem of tribal justice. Lack of professionalism and legal knowledge throughout the tribal justice system result in a situation in which essentially groundless or illegal arrests, charges, and even convictions become commonplace. According to this lawyer: "If I don't like you and want to get you, all I have to do is call the tribal police and tell them I want you arrested. I can have you in jail at the drop of a hat—nobody knows anything about probable cause. I can simply say that you were bothering me or that you insulted me or my wife or something."

be gathered, all that took place was that the accused threatened to "beat up" the complainant because the latter had accused the former of breaking a window in his home. An arrest and criminal charge on the basis of this allegation are excessive if not plainly unlawful; but the advocate, who is not trained in the law and in concepts of sufficient or probable cause, fails to perceive it. Later, when speaking in private, the advocate admits being frustrated by his lack of legal ability. Though not stating it explicitly, he implies that the only role he can play is an obstructionist one—making life difficult for the judges. Still, that is not wholly negative: it may help keep the judges on their toes about trial rights, however misdirected the specific motions and questions may be. Moreover, some psychological benefit appears to be transmitted to defendants so represented. It is not much, and it affects only few cases (the vast majority of defendants still go unrepresented). Also, the advocate's reputation on Standing Rock Reservation is not too favorable; by some, he is dismissed as a loudmouthed, uneducated radical. (Since my visit to the reservation, he has been banned from further "practice" in the court by the new judicial administration.)[70]

It is relevant here to cite the commentary of one tribal official (an Indian and member of the tribe). Though it is very harsh, it suggests a possible solution to problems of justice on the reservation. This informant's general opinion was that the tribal court was "pathetic" and in need of a "complete overhaul," to which he added: "What we need is nothing 'racial'—we need just plain white man's justice with no consideration of 'extenuating circumstances.' We just need strict 'law and order' around here."

One way in which an element of "white man's justice" was brought into the Standing Rock tribal court was through the periodic visits of the lawyer-judge from Lemmon. The instance I observed (the bottle-throwing case) resulted in an acquittal, which would not have squared with the Indian commentator's expectations of "white justice." But with the facts being presented as they were and the case being tried before a jury, this was the only possible outcome. The lawyer-judge confined

---

70. Telephone conversation with the advocate.

himself to addressing an occasional question or request for clari-
fication to the witnesses and to keeping the lay advocate under
control, both of which he did effectively enough. There were no
shouting scenes or arguments among the litigants or between the
advocate and the opposing party or judge, as there had been
when the Indian judges presided. Later observations of the
performance of the visiting judge on the Fort Totten Reservation (detailed in the appendix) confirmed a good impression of
this arrangement. Significantly, the Indian people seem on the
whole to favor the experience with "professional" justice. When
asked their opinion about having a white lawyer play judge in an
Indian court, the common reservation people respond as follows:
"At least he goes by the books," and "He knows what he's
doing—he's got the education." They also imply or express a
strong respect for independence as well as education, and serious
misgivings about the Indian judges whom they perceive as having
neither. The politicians and tribal judges on Standing Rock,
however, are less enthusiastic about the setup. Rightly, in one
sense, they ask what is "Indian" or "tribal" about a court that
employs white lawyers as judges. But, then, what is "Indian"
about the tribal laws and procedures or the courtroom itself and
its clanking radiators? In any event, on Standing Rock Reservation the white lawyer-judge system was already on the way out.

THE BLACKFEET SYSTEM

The Blackfeet Reservation is located in northwestern
Montana. Its western boundary runs along the eastern edge of
Glacier National Park, a beautiful area of mountains, lakes, and
forests. The reservation proper encompasses only the eastern
foothills of the Glacier National Park mountains (Lewis Range)
and thus only a minute portion of the area's timber, water,
wildlife (and tourist) resources.

Most of the reservation land is barren, treeless, rolling plain
with significant relief only where small rivers cut deeply into the
landscape. Approaching the reservation from the west—that is,
through Glacier National Park—one is struck by the dramatic
change in landscape from the spectacularly majestic and green to
the drab and brown. It is difficult to escape a pang of guilt: this
is what the white man did to the Indian; this is what he left
him. A more sobering approach is from the east, where one has

to traverse endless stretches of plains—wheatfields or grazing country—until, nearing the eastern boundaries of the reservation, one begins to perceive with some clarity the mountains on the western horizon. The dominant thought then may be that at least the Blackfeet live in the shadow of a beautiful area, which is more than can be said for most inhabitants of the northern plains. Another comforting consideration may be that the Black-feet tribes are essentially and historically plains Indians; though clearly dispossessed and otherwise disadvantaged by the advance of white civilization, they have not been "transformed" from a mountain people into a plains people.[71]

Today, the Blackfeet—whatever their traditional habitat or means of livelihood—live a typical reservation existence. That is, the majority are gathered in the few towns scattered around the reservation, where jobs are mostly government related (tribal and federal) or service oriented (motels, gas stations, tourist shops, and the like) catering to transients. Not much of the land is used. The wheatfields to the east pretty much disappear at the reservation proper.[72] Grazing occurs in small-scale fashion. If it is done on a larger scale, it is only sporadic and scattered, often—though certainly not always—conducted by whites who own or lease reservation property. The Blackfeet in the western-most portion of the reservation engage in some forestry and hunting and fishing, but these pursuits involve comparatively few people on any regular basis.

The total Indian population of the reservation is around 5,500-6,000. Browning, the "capital," accounts for some 1,700 people; the rest are distributed among small settlements like Babb, Kiowa, Blackfoot, Heart Butte, Saint Mary, and East

---

71. Even if there had been such a transformation, as an incidental by-product of the white conquest, it is not clear what moral assessment should be made. The history of the Indian tribes is filled with such occurrences, both before and after the advent of the whites on the continent. The Navajo, Apache, Kiowa—many of the major tribes—have well-preserved oral histories of migrations, conquests, and defeats in warfare; economic and social adaptation to new environments; cultural borrowing from new neighbors; and the like that go back long before the spread of Spanish and Anglo civilization caused further transformations. On the other hand, there is something particularly tragic in the few "forced" (and unsuccessful) attempts by shortsighted white policy makers to turn Indian hunters or fishermen into instant Christian farmers.

72. See notes 25 and 62 *supra*.

Glacier, with "populations" officially listed as ranging from as low as 15 to a maximum of 400. Because of the reservation's proximity to Glacier National Park, tourists are a common sight during the summer months. Since most drive through, and those who stop often do so only to fill up on gas or to browse through the few curio shops, the economic benefits to the reservation are marginal. Browning, essentially a ramshackle, depressed-looking town with only one "respectable" motel, testifies to this fact. To some extent, it may also be a cause of it. In the winter months, Browning ceases even to be a thoroughfare. The climate is extreme: dry, with hot summers and cold winters and with temperature variations within seasons, days, or even hours which genuinely merit the term phenomenal. Erratic mountain winds can bring warm, Pacific air streaming over the ranges from the west or at other times blow frigid, arctic air from north-northwesterly directions paralleling the slopes.

The Blackfeet tribal court is located in an unimpressive law-and-order building at the northern edge of the town of Browning. It has the reputation of being a "good" court among white "Indian experts," who are apologetic about the shape of the Standing Rock tribal court specifically, but sold on the tribal court *concept.* They imply that the Standing Rock situation is unrepresentatively negative and that the Blackfeet system, perhaps unusually favorable, holds out the promise of how well tribal courts can ideally work.

It may be instructive to take a look at the operations of a court with such a favorable reputation. Why does it have this reputation? Is it deserved? One immediate comment is that the favorable reputation is exclusively an off-reservation phenomenon. Within the Blackfeet Reservation, the court is viewed with about the same mixture of cynicism and apathy as that encountered on Standing Rock (and later elsewhere). The men-in-the-street, the defendants, the tribal police[73] the council members, the administrative assistants, and even the associate

---

73. The chief of police repeatedly complained about getting "stabbed in the back" by the tribal court. For example, the nephew of a tribal council member had been arrested for drunkenness and assaulting a police officer: "Next thing you know the council member calls up the court, and the guy (arrestee) is walking out of the [law-and-order] building before we'd finished booking him."

judges themselves, none had much of anything favorable to say about the operations of the Blackfeet court. Several expressed their criticism openly, while others showed their cynicism more implicitly in the way they acted on, and talked about, their court-connected jobs. About the only commentary to the contrary came from the chief judge of the court: although he was aware of the problems, he usually spoke about the court operations in relatively hopeful and positive terms.

Statistics on the Blackfeet court operations were presented earlier (see page 32 above). One recalls that the crime and disposition patterns were quite similar to those of Standing Rock. A distinct feature was that the Blackfeet were seen to handle under the category of "disorderly conduct" much of what appeared as "drunkenness" in the Standing Rock compilations— not a substantive difference. In comparison with Standing Rock, there was heavier enforcement in traffic cases, but one suspected that the difference was in enforcement only and not in actual driving patterns.

Despite minor differences, the dispensation of justice was basically similar on the Blackfeet and Standing Rock reservations.

One conceivable reason for the good off-reservation reputation of the Blackfeet court may be that it has a personnel and agency-supporting structure not unlike white courts. Aiding the court, which is made up of a chief judge and two associate judges, are a prosecutor, court administrator, and juvenile officer as well as a defense organization and probation department. These resources are often missing on other reservations. In addition, like the state courts, the Blackfeet court is divided into (at least nominally) separate branches for criminal, civil, juvenile, and small claims cases. In fact, the avowed aspiration of the chief judge is that the court be "just like the regular [white] courts." On all the reservations I visited, the goal of the tribal court officials was to duplicate what were believed to be the features of the regular court system. The more one saw of tribal justice, however, the more one wondered whether such duplication efforts could ever be successful or even appropriate: whether they could "work," could "make sense," and would mean "better justice" for the reservation Indians. The courts often observed the forms of the outside system without understanding their purpose. As the result, such observance sometimes was at the expense of substantive justice.

One case in which the Blackfeet court attempted to emulate the white system resulted in a default judgment. Thereafter the chief judge was to proudly and repeatedly cite the decision as proof that the Blackfeet court was a "real" court, one with teeth and everything. The case was in the tribal small claims court, which means that the amount in controversy was relatively small. Otherwise, the laws and procedures, the personnel and the place where the proceedings were held were indistinguishable from those for any other case (in itself a signal of somewhat less than meaningful emulation). On hearing about the judgment, the losing party was furious and came to argue with the judge for an hour, to no avail. What is bothersome is that the judge's own version of the case indicates that the individual labored under some genuine misapprehension—clearly misapprehension of the court's power under the circumstances and, more seriously, perhaps misapprehension of whether or when his appearance was required. Penalizing the unwitting is surely not the purpose behind the power of courts to render default judgments. Particularly on the reservation, where most people have little grasp of court power and processes and are unaided by counsel, the possibility of genuine ignorance is high, and the opportunity for curing it is readily available (the losing party in the instant case was available enough to come to argue with the judge).[74]

In another case, an 18-year-old boy was charged with several counts, which included car theft, drunken driving, wrecking stolen property, and leaving the scene of an accident. As each count was formally read off to the accused, his Indian lay advocate moved for dismissal of the charge because the arresting officer was not in court. After checking with the Indian lay prosecutor for possible arguments against dismissal, the judge granted each motion. The accused himself never spoke during these very formal and properly conducted proceedings.

Some background facts later emerged, however, which led one

---

74. A similar action and attitude were encountered in the Navajo court, where the judges boasted about a case that had resulted in a $54,000 default judgment.

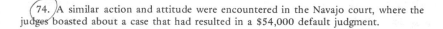

to wonder whether under the circumstances the insistence on formality and regularity made sense. As it turned out, everyone involved in the case knew the police officer would not show up; nonetheless, the proceedings were held instead of being rescheduled. The officer's failure to appear had to do with a long-standing dispute among the tribal council, court, and police department. Earlier that year, the police had been on strike for higher wages for several months when a new tribal council came to power and proceeded to try to end the dispute by firing "almost the entire police force." That this was no solution became quickly apparent, and many of the more experienced officers were hired back and wage demands were partially met. But those who were not rehired, and some of those who were, continued the fight by refusing to cooperate with the court, refusing to appear, and using other such tactics.

Despite these demonstrations of so-perceived white ways in the tribal court, the chief judge also talks much about the need to "go slow in terms of upgrading procedures, so you don't confuse the people." In some ways and on some issues, this is a valid consideration. On the other hand, the chief judge's expressed opposition to allowing white professional lawyers in the tribal court and his general misgivings about other Civil Rights Act provisions may reflect self-concern or self-doubt as much as concern for "the people."

One afternoon, while the court commission of the tribal council is meeting in the courtroom, an unscheduled arraignment takes place in the court clerk's office of three mixed-blood cowboys who are charged with trespassing on private property. The three men stand around or lean against the wall; they are outdoor types, dressed as if they have just come from a roundup. The judge sits, and the prosecutor moves about the office. Proceedings begin with the judge's reading off the rights at trial and making the men sign a piece of paper stating that they have been so advised. The men plead not guilty and indicate a preference for hiring their own attorney and having a jury trial. At that point, the hearing turns quite informal, with the judge stating explicitly that he is talking "as a friend, no longer as a judge." In a fairly mild way, he tries to talk the men out of their jury demand; whether he is successful is unclear, since the three accused remain noncommittal. Some of the details of the case begin to emerge. The complainant in the case is an elderly and respected woman; her claim is that by running cattle through her garden the men did more than $500 damage. A question is raised and remains unresolved about whether the eventual trial will be in the nature of a civil or criminal action, or whether it will be some hybrid proceeding. Despite these vagaries, the proceedings impress favorably: there seems to be the proper balance between regularity and informality and between authority on the part of the court and respect shown for that authority on the part of the defendants. It is that kind of atmosphere and procedure which one would hope to find characteristic of local tribal justice. Duplication of (white) court formalities has little to do with the quest to achieve such a balance.

The following morning I have the opportunity to observe the rare event of a fully contested trial. Unfortunately, it exposes the weaknesses of the Blackfeet system.

The accused in this case are two rough-looking half-bloods and their girl friends. All four are charged with assault and battery on the basis of a complaint filed by a young couple—a white man of about 25 and his attractive, well-dressed Indian wife. Even before the case begins, some irregularities show up. In the presence of an outside observer, the tribal judge and prosecutor freely talk about their perceptions of the defendants as "real troublemakers." Then the prosecutor asks the judge at what point it would be best to bring in alleged "evidence" that the defendants have offered to "pay off" the complainants if they drop the case. The judge's answer is to the effect that it is up to the prosecutor himself; subsequently at the trial, as described below, the latter proceeds to introduce this evidence in a very ingenious fashion.

After the proceedings have been formally opened, the prosecutor begins by motioning to have all witnesses removed from the courtroom, including, as he later confides, his "surprise" witness. The associate judge who is presiding over the case grants the motion, and everyone files out of the courtroom, even the defendants. Shortly, however, one of the two Indian lay "public defenders" realizes that something is amiss and succeeds in having at least the defendants brought back in the courtroom.

The trial then begins in earnest. Organizationally, it is a total jumble, though this is probably the least of its problems. One male defender defends one of the females accused; the other defender, an Indian woman of around 50, has the other three. The male defender calls no witnesses other than the defendant herself; in his "final statement," he will base this neglect on the fact that the female defender was to present the defense witnesses. Meanwhile, however, the prosecutor has been handling everything as separate cases, which has resulted in an irritating repetition of pseudoformalities (swearing in and so forth) and much duplicated testimony. After a while, however, all participants tire of this, and a consensus is reached to try at least the male defendants as one case.

Throughout the trial the associate judge makes various interjections and rulings which seem designed more to assert his authority than to have a substantive effect on the trial. In reality, the proceedings are out of the judge's control, organizationally *and* substantively.

It is the prosecutor who actually runs the court and gets away with some questionable tactics. Without objection or censure, for example, he presents "evidence" (by simply announcing it in the form of a question asked of the defendants) that other people involved in the alleged fight have been convicted in the court of a neighboring county, although this is neither relevant to nor probative of anything. He dismisses the testimony of defendants and defense witnesses by simply stating, without foundation or provocation, that they have prior criminal records and are variously "related" to one another. As "evidence" of the payoff offer that was allegedly made by the accused to the complainants, the prosecutor simply states it as a fact while one of the complainants is on the witness stand. And finally he springs the "surprise" witness. This woman—a friend of the plaintiffs—has nothing startling to offer in substance, but her appearance—as a tactic—clearly unsettles the public defender, who gets up and walks up to the judge saying, "What does this do to my case? What does this do to my case?" A brief conference is held then, during which the public defender is assured that it does not matter very much.[75]

---

75. During this conference the judge asked me for advice on the issue. In an unrelated case, the same judge asked whether forfeiture of bond meant that the

More typically, however, the defenders and court fail to respond to, or contain, the prosecutor altogether. When it comes time for the defense to present its case, this failing becomes most apparent. As mentioned earlier, the male defender's case consists solely of putting one of the defendants on the stand and essentially having her give her version of the incident. The female defender's case is more elaborate but in substance no more adequate. In fact, she clearly inhibits the defendants, who would probably be better off conducting the defense themselves. As it is, they have to coach her; they tell her which witnesses to call; they react visibly to the prosecutor's excesses. But she only listens to half of what they try to tell her. Mostly she goes her own way, very slowly, speaking very timidly. She asks each witness, including the defendants, one question:

> You are in court here for [she names the defendants]. You are under oath and you must tell the truth. Would you tell the court what you saw on the night of August 25 at the [names a reservation bar] about the fight between [the defendants and the complaining witnesses]?

The fight she refers to is one the existence of which the defendants seek to deny.

It is later learned that the female defender used to be a tribal court judge herself. But, in the words of one informant, she was an old-time moralist who "really threw the book at everybody," so eventually "the council got rid of her." Now she is one of the officially designated lay advocates upon whom defendants in the Blackfeet tribal court must depend. The male defender observed in action was a bit more verbal, but he, too, lacked real competence, real confidence, or credibility. All the proceedings in the Blackfeet tribal court are conducted in English. One court official suggested that part of the female defender's problem was that she spoke English poorly.

The performance of the same defenders in a series of arraignment proceedings the following morning is no better. This time it is the typical tribal court scene: about 15-20 accused are

person who had forfeited could no longer be prosecuted. These and similar occurrences on other reservations show the seriousness of the lack of legal knowledge and the way it affects even comparatively simple cases and issues.

waiting to be arraigned. The majority are older, alcohol-ravaged
men; almost all are shaking very badly; 2 or 3 can hardly walk,
and several appear to be almost deaf. It is a discouraging sight to
see these men dealt with in "criminal" proceedings in a court:
their problems are so clearly nonlegal, or at least noncriminal.
All the cases amount to fighting, drunkenness, disorderly conduct, resisting arrest, and the like. The chief judge, who is
conducting the proceedings, and the court clerk make a good
effort to inform the accused of their rights and the charges
against them. For several, however, it is simply to no avail. They
are physically unable to see and to hear, and the process itself is
fundamentally irrelevant to their predicament. All except 2 of
the accused either plead guilty immediately or are (gently)
persuaded to do so. In the 5 or so cases in which he is involved,
the male defender pleads guilty on behalf of his client, then
argues, like a social worker, for the client's commitment to an
off-reservation rehabilitation center. The judge's response to this
tactic is that it is no longer possible for tribal court to commit
reservation residents to the state "detox" centers now that the
reservation has its own center. This makeshift and overcrowded
reservation center, however, has no medical or other professional
personnel of any kind. The home for the aged is a possibility,
but most of the men do not want to go there. So if they are
able to pay the fine out of their welfare check, they wind up
back on the street, and no doubt back in jail in a day or so.
One finds such scenes in the non-Indian urban courts, of course.
But it seems both unnecessary and contrary to the basic objectives behind tribal autonomy that the phenomenon of mass,
summary processing should operate with such vengeance in local
rural reservation courts.

Lack of preparation on the part of the defense is also a problem. In a case involving a younger Indian man, a misunderstand-
ing develops between the defender and the accused about what
the plea is to be. After a short recess, the defender pleads guilty
on behalf of the client. In another case, the chief judge more or
less forces a continuance on the defender when the latter is
unable to get his client's facts straight about the origin of a set
of license plates which are at the heart of the matter. Though it
is a good move by the judge, it makes the defender look bad.

The relative strengths and weaknesses of the prosecution and

defense vary from reservation to reservation. On the Blackfeet
Reservation, the prosecution dominates, not because it is strong
but because the defense is weak. On other reservations (e.g., the
Navajo), a reverse situation holds, with defense services generally
outmatching a prosecutorial branch that is weak (or sometimes
nonexistent). (The least fortunate reservations are unable to provide representation for either side.) Imbalance in the courts is
further caused or aggravated by the weakness of most of the
tribal judges. With little experience or training and with a perception of their role which is too limited, the tribal judges are
generally unable to bring balance to, or maintain control over,
proceedings.

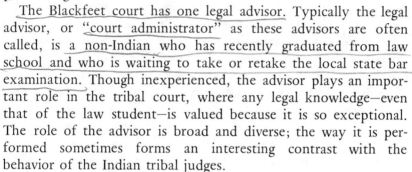

The Blackfeet court has one legal advisor. Typically the legal
advisor, or "court administrator" as these advisors are often
called, is a non-Indian who has recently graduated from law
school and who is waiting to take or retake the local state bar
examination. Though inexperienced, the advisor plays an important role in the tribal court, where any legal knowledge—even
that of the law student—is valued because it is so exceptional.
The role of the advisor is broad and diverse; the way it is per-
formed sometimes forms an interesting contrast with the
behavior of the Indian tribal judges.

One morning I was able to observe the legal advisor in action
in a preliminary hearing on a civil dispute involving land leased
for grazing to a white cattle rancher. The disputants are two
Indian couples, each claiming the land and the rental fee of
$200. The rancher is caught in the middle. It is the complexity
of the problem that has led to the preliminary handling and the
involvement of the court advisor, who normally, as on other
reservations, would not become involved in litigation. The Indian
parties are yelling at and threatening each other, and occasionally their fire is directed at the rancher, who is told that his
cattle will be impounded or that other drastic measures will be
taken. Although the argumentation is heated, none of it is taken
too seriously by the advisor, who apparently views it as cathartic
and not necessarily inappropriate at a preliminary proceeding. It
does not help resolve the dispute though. After a while, a local
BIA official who works in the land-records department, is
brought in. Perhaps owing to lack of preparation, he can shed
no light on the problem either. This gives the youthfully

"radical" advisor an opportunity to make some snide remarks about the BIA in general. The proceedings then threaten to bog down again into more meaningless charges and countercharges until the rancher himself comes up with the solution. He suggests that he will "pay the $200 into the bank," after which the disputants can continue to fight over it. The court advisor, recognizing a solution when one is presented, takes up on this and starts throwing the word "escrow" around. Pretty soon, all parties—accompanied by the advisor—are peacefully on their way to the bank.

While it may have left something to be desired, the contribution of the advisor should not be too readily minimized. A good deal of seemingly undirected bickering was allowed to go on; at the same time, the advisor provided a legal focus and relevant constraints and ultimately put the "solution" into what was perceived by all to be an acceptable legal framework. Even if primarily symbolic and semantic, this kind of contribution of expertise is often what the disputing parties are looking for, and it is generally more than the untrained tribal judges can provide.

Other aspects of the advisor's job performance also have a major symbolic quality. As distinct from involvement in the resolution of an individual case, these aspects are more politically and public relations oriented, and their value is more dubious. Recent non-Indian law school graduates are not particularly well equipped for dabbling in tribal politics or assuming the complex responsibilities of lawmaking. This, however, is essentially what they are doing when, as here on the Blackfeet Reservation and elsewhere as well, they become involved in drawing up tribal court "bar examinations," tribal code and constitutional "revisions," officious "appellate" opinions, and the like. Potentially, the consequences of these activities can be far-reaching, and not necessarily positive, given the advisors' limited experience and foresight. What it often boils down to is this: the young advisors—that is, their knowledge of law, or more precisely, their knowledge of legal language—are being exploited by tribal politicians for purposes which may benefit the politicians but which are of questionable value to the tribal courts, the reservation people, or the advisors themselves.

THE NAVAJO SYSTEM

The Navajo Reservation, or Navajo Nation as it prefers to be identified these days, contains by far the largest Indian tribe in the United States. With an area of some 34,000 square miles (about the size of West Virginia) and a population variously estimated between 100,000 and 146,000,[76] which is close to one-half of the total United States Indian reservation population, the Navajo tribe cannot be overlooked in a study of Indian institutions, but paradoxically perhaps, neither can the Navajo situation be viewed as representative of what takes place on Indian reservations. The Navajo tribe does not face some of the predicaments of the typically small and sparsely populated reservations. On the other hand, it may have problems that are not found among other tribes.

The Navajo Reservation is located at the "four-corners" area where the state boundaries of Arizona, New Mexico, Colorado, and Utah meet. By far the largest portion of the reservation is in northeastern Arizona, with comparatively small areas extending into New Mexico and Utah. The Hopi Indian Reservation is located right in the middle of Navajo country in Arizona, which means that the two groups are involved in frequent disputes over landownership and grazing rights. The Hopi, incidentally, are—anthropologically speaking—a Pueblo Indian group that is indigenous to the Southwest, whereas the Navajo, like the Apaches, were originally a northwestern tribe, which migrated to the Southwest perhaps as late as the thirteenth century A.D. Thus, between the Navajo and Hopi, there are lingering frictions and differences of a cultural origin in addition to the concrete modern-day disputes.[77] Outside the well-defined outer bound-

76. The 146,000 figure is from tribal sources—funding applications and annual reports—and is almost certainly too high. Perhaps the ulterior motive of obtaining financial support for various tribal enterprises and services results in the inclusion of non-Indian reservation residents or off-reservation tribal members (of whom there are many) in the count of reservation Indians. The 100,000 figure—the lower extreme—is from 7 Encyclopaedia Britannica (Micropaedia) 227-28 (1974); see also 16 Encyclopaedia Britannica 172E (1962). Encyclopaedia Britannica is also one of the sources for some of the other descriptive information in this section.

77. It is easy to overestimate, as the Indians themselves are wont to do, the significance of the historic cultural differences. Today, by and large, the "cultural" similarities among the tribes outweigh the old distinctions. In the minds of many Indians, however, the old distinctions often continue to loom large. The Hopi feel very different from the Navajo; the Sioux still despise the Chippewa, and vice versa, for a variety of social and historical reasons; the Blackfeet still look down on the Crow Indians because the latter collaborated with the whites during the nineteenth-century "wars" on the high plains; and so on. At least, the Indians often like to take such postures. For some tribes or individuals it may not go much beyond that; for others, it is a more genuine matter.

aries of the Navajo Reservation is a checkerboard area of white
and Indian landholdings, the center of which is Crown Point,
New Mexico. The Navajo prefer to put this area on their maps
as part of the reservation proper. Finally, in New Mexico there
are three small settlements completely detached from any reservation lands which are predominantly Navajo and under Navajo
government.

The entire Navajo region is quite arid; the high plateaus
receive somewhat more than average (for the area) rainfall, but
the lower regions are parched. The effects of variable precipita-
tion can be clearly observed in the vegetation, which ranges
from pine forest (exceptional) to shrub and brush country (typical) to total desert (less typical). Temperatures vary with eleva-
tion, of course: overall, however, the reservation lies at a relatively high altitude, a fact that makes for summers that are a lot
more pleasant than those in the lower elevations of Arizona
(e.g., the Phoenix area) and for winters that have occasionally
severe days and especially nights.

Among the "traditional"[78] Navajo pursuits that are still
carried out today are small-time farming and especially the herding of sheep, goats, and cattle. Because of the aridity of the
region, however, these pursuits cannot supply a livelihood for
everyone, and many Navajo earn their livings as transient
workers in places outside the reservation, such as Gallup, Holbrook, Winslow, Flagstaff, and Farmington. Some have even set-
tled in these towns, and others have moved so far as to settle on
irrigated lands along the lower Colorado River or in urban centers like Phoenix and Los Angeles. Other economically significant on-reservation pursuits are silversmithing (probably first
learned from Mexican smiths in the middle of the nineteenth
century), and weaving, pottery making, and dry-sand painting
(arts learned from the Pueblo). A few heavy-industry plants have
been established on the reservation, and more are projected.
Then there is, of course, the usual number of tribal and federal
government jobs; and for the rest, unemployment.

---

78. Traditional to the extent that these means of livelihood developed before
contact with Anglo-whites, but *after* contact with the Pueblo Indians and the Spanish.
Originally, the Navajo were hunters and fishermen in the northwestern regions of the
North American continent.

In some ways the Navajo remain a comparatively "traditional" people. Their tribal language remains a vital force: in fact, a good percentage of the older and more rural population speaks little or no English; on the other hand, substantial numbers among the younger generation, more urbanized and more educated, speak little or no Navajo. Court proceedings on the Navajo Reservation are often conducted in the tribal language, sometimes in English, and frequently in a mixture of both. Ceremonial dances and gatherings are still regular occurrences, although it may be difficult to label such affairs as "traditional." Reportedly, the medicine man still exerts power and influence over some of the older and less acculturated Navajo, and clan and family bonds remain a factor to be reckoned with in many contexts (as is the case on virtually all reservations, which may indicate that it is not so much a function of culture and tradition as it is a by-product of the fact that reservations are more or less closed societies). On the other hand, there are also indications that the Navajo are becoming more acculturated and more urbanized. Today a large part of the population resides in towns of 700-900 inhabitants (Window Rock, Shiprock, Crown Point, Fort Defiance, Chinle, Kayenta, Tuba City, etc.)—tiny settlements by eastern standards but not nearly so insignificant in the sparsely populated Southwest—in contrast with the earlier days when families lived in earthen or log hogans miles removed from the nearest neighbor. Of course, an ever increasing influx of the trappings of white "culture" surrounds and affects the Navajo: motels, drug stores, gas stations, curio shops, industrial plants, liquor, automobiles, radios, television sets, rock music, and so on. A comparatively small and encircled society can remain "traditional" for only so long in the face of such a cultural onslaught.

Compared with the courts of the other reservations, the Navajo tribal court presents the best "appearance of justice," both in terms of the manner in which proceedings are conducted and in terms of staffing and facilities to operate the system and implement its decisions. Administratively, court operations seemed to be well under control, on my first visit at any rate. Proceedings were held regularly and with reasonable punctuality; a strong sense of decorum pervaded, and most defendants seemed to regard the tribal judges with respect (and, one thought, even fear). Physical facilities, compared with the situation on other reservations, were more than adequate, although the Navajo chief justice complained much to the contrary. Clerical help and technological gadgetry—film, microphones, sound recorders—were in relatively abundant supply. An impressive library, containing a professionally bound and printed tribal code, and well-kept court records occupied several rooms in the main court building in Window Rock. Two young legally trained court advisors—one white and one Navajo—helped out on legal and administrative detail but played no role in the trial of cases. Several law students doing a variety of court-related jobs circulated on the premises. The chief justice enjoyed the luxury of confining himself to administrative work and appeals, leaving trials to the six trial judges. Appeals, when granted, resulted in formal opinions, which were published in annual reports. This procedure was unheard of on the other reservations. A police force, led by a specially recruited and financed white police chief, operated out of offices on the ground floor of the Window Rock law-and-order building, one wing of which was designated as the police academy. The courtrooms and offices were on the second floor and the jail in the basement. Two large and well-funded organizations handled defense functions: Navajo Legal Aid Services and DNA.[79] Each organization operated out of offices separate from the law-and-order building, and each had several white professional attorneys in its employ. The DNA, a group with a national reputation, also had a large auxiliary staff of Navajo "paralegals." Although it was not as well endowed, the prosecutorial department had enough funds (in theory) to allow for a chief prosecutor and one or two assistants in each of the five (or six)[80] court districts on the Navajo Reservation. (Some reservations had no prosecutor at all.) Full-time trial judges operated in each of the district courts of Window Rock, Shiprock, Crown Point, Chinle, Tuba City (and Kayenta). The DNA defense organization had representatives in each of the districts and maintained relatively large and impres-

---

79. DNA stands for *Dinebeiina Nahiilna Be Agaditahe*, Navajo for "Lawyers for the Development of the People."

80. At the time of the fieldwork, the operational existence of the sixth district court in Kayenta was in doubt.

sive offices in Window Rock and Shiprock. In addition, leaders within DNA were in the process of setting up a Navajo bar association and a bar examination geared to paralegals.

Despite the outward appearances, the Navajo court system was plagued with many of the same problems that existed in the tribal courts of other reservations, albeit to a lesser degree than in the least advantaged ones. In some instances, the favorable personnel situation in the Navajo system was literally a paper advantage only. As mentioned earlier, in 1975 resignations and retirements had left only three trial judges to cover the six court districts. This was a temporary situation and no doubt exceptional in its paralyzing effect on the Navajo court operations. On the other hand, the perpetuation or recurrence of comparable if perhaps less drastic situations seemed inevitable, since there was no indication that the underlying conditions causing the vacancies—low stature and low pay—could be remedied. Other court and court-related staffs suffered from similar problems. Prosecutorial positions were vacant in a couple of districts and had to be filled by personnel traveling in from other districts as far as 75-100 miles away. The same was true for positions in probation, parole, and juvenile offices. The very significant defense services available on the Navajo Reservation, particularly DNA, were also hampered by turnover and vacancies. Of the 75-80 lay advocates listed as working with professional backup help in the Navajo courts, for example, it turned out that fewer than 20 were currently active. Finally, as on all other reservations, the tribal judges, prosecutors, probation people, and Indian advocates were handicapped by lack of legal training or much formal or secondary education of any kind. And there were indications that the plans for a tribal bar association and bar examination threatened to become self-serving schemes whose primary objectives would be to keep out white professionals while augmenting the status and power of the nonprofessional.

The practical results are by now familiar from the descriptions of operations on other reservations. As implied in the statistical material presented earlier, lack of genuine, balanced fact-finding and contest are as typical a pattern on the Navajo Reservation as elsewhere. Summary justice, with high rates for guilty-pleas, convictions, and winning plaintiffs, is as much the essence of the Navajo court scene as of the courts of other reservations, and with little more justification. In nine days of observation in the Navajo courts, I saw only one fully contested criminal case, one aborted one, and two consensual civil judgments (cattle ownership and grazing rights). The rest of the time, I observed the routine of defendants making guilty pleas without information or advice and being given quick fines or sentences.

But it was precisely at the preliminary arraignment stage that the vast majority of issues, and issues of consequence, were decided. It was there that neither DNA nor Navajo Legal Aid provided any representation. It was there that the poorer drunks were fined and jailed, while those with some money walked out. It was there that a woman defendant charged with a drinking-related traffic offense and unable to meet high bail was returned to the lockup. It was there that one could observe stiff fines and sometimes sentences handed out routinely, with little to no premeditation on the part of anyone and, to judge from the recidivism rates, with no more correctional effect. It was there that one learned that a 16-year-old Navajo girl whose "offense" was that her mother found her unmanageable was detained in jail.

The common reservation court problems of lack of authority and lack of confidence on the part of the judges, their lack of independence from reservation politics, and the lack of respect for them on the part of the residents also surfaced in the Navajo courts, though in more subtle terms than on a reservation like Standing Rock. It is true that defendants were uniformly respectful and that young advocates—lay and professional, Indian and non-Indian—usually made supportive statements about tribal justice to the effect that it was probably no worse and was perhaps better than local non-Indian justice (about which they knew little or nothing firsthand). There were also counter-indications, however. Often the advocates' underlying contempt for the tribal judges showed through when they responded to questions about judicial performance or independence with only a sarcastic smile or answered a question concerning the whereabouts of a certain judge who did not show up as scheduled with "He's probably out fishing." Most seriously, their fundamental cynicism about the court was demonstrated in the way they exploited the lack of legal ability of the judges and other functionaries in the tribal justice system; on cue from their professional backup lawyers or on the basis of their own knowledge of such tactics, they succeeded in having the majority of the cases they handled dismissed immediately[81] or otherwise resolved in their favor on the basis of legal technicalities.

On the Navajo Reservation, prosecution and defense services are rendered in cases that go to trial (some 10 percent of the caseload) and cases heard on appeal (76 in 1974). Appeals, while handled formally, remain a problematic part of tribal justice, as elsewhere. Both the decision to hear an appeal and the ruling on the merits are entirely within the discretion of the chief justice. The result is a small and select appellate load. The prosecutor of one of the two major judicial districts complained about not having been granted a single appeal over a period of more than a year, despite repeated petitions. Invariably he was rebuffed on technical grounds. This situation appears to support the virtually unanimous view that the defense outmatches the prosecution in the Navajo system. The reason lies in the fact that the defense has more resources, human and financial. Compared with Navajo Legal Aid and DNA, the prosecution is essentially a neglected function; its overburdened and rather demoralized staff is made up of nonprofessionals; it has no training program; and, as on other reservations, it is not really independent from the judicial branch.[82]

I was able to observe a case that illustrates well the lack of balance between defense and prosecution as well as the absence of court control: After an incident allegedly involving police brutality, a charge of resisting arrest is filed in the tribal court against a Navajo civilian and a charge of assault with a deadly weapon is lodged in the federal court against the police officer (also a Navajo). In the tribal court case, which is of primary concern here, the citizen-defendant is represented by a young

---

81. See, e.g., the police brutality case described below. Statistically, of the roughly 10 percent of the total cases that are contested, about 40 percent result in findings of guilty, 10 percent in findings of not guilty, and 40 percent in dismissals. Advocates reportedly participate in most, but not all, of the contested cases.

82. One of the defense organizations is involved in off-reservation and non-Indian work as well, which is not separated from the Indian, reservation business. As a result, it is impossible to make a meaningful comparison between the defense and prosecution budgets on the reservation. Suffice it to say that reports show that the combined financial resources of the defense organizations are at least seven times larger than the budget for the prosecutors.

white attorney, while the prosecution is handled by an Indian lay prosecutor. The actual proceedings, contrary to their potential, are anticlimatic and unsatisfactory. The primary witness to the incident, a tribal police officer already suspended from the force as a result of the incident, has not shown up despite being subpoenaed. The white defense lawyer moves for a dismissal and gets it. It does not occur to the court or the prosecution to have the case continued until the witness can be produced, and the defender and his client walk out of the courtroom triumphantly, accepting a handshake here and there from various court assistants and defense organization personnel whose sympathies are fashionably antipolice.[83]

The case shows that it is too easy for the party with the somewhat more clever or slightly better trained representative to get away with too much. Informants on the police force complained of numerous similar instances in which cases were dismissed because of a misguided application of some misunderstood technicality—a name may have been misspelled, an identification census number may have been missing, a charge may have been communicated by the wrong official at the wrong moment, and so forth. The advocates on the Navajo Reservation—lay or professional—operate in a strict adversary fashion, without considering the weaknesses or imbalances of the system. They represent the interests of their clients and themselves only. In some settings—the outside legal world—one may argue that this is the way it should be. It is more difficult to sustain the argument in a reservation court setting, where lay judges and untrained prosecutors and police officers are trying to deal with major social and criminal problems.[84] To be sure, the tribal

---

83. A mini-war is taking place between one of the defense attorneys and the chief of the tribal police (both white) over the issue of police brutality. Both sides engage in some tinkering with the facts and other excesses. The situation is no doubt complex, with the merits of individual incidents only barely reflected in the general positions taken. Owing to lack of sufficient information, it is impossible to take sides on the issue; it is clear, as is usual in such disputes, that individual police officers and private citizens are caught in the middle and are used as pawns by the disputing parties.

84. One of the more serious examples of the excesses of professional lawyers in the tribal courts comes from one of the North Dakota reservations that I did not study in depth. Reports from several sources permit reconstruction of the following incident: An Indian student was dismissed from an off-reservation high school track team for unspecified disciplinary reasons. A regional Legal Services lawyer took up the cause, bringing an action in the tribal court against the local school board to force it

police and prosecution have their excesses. The trouble is that even they get away with most of them when, despite being indiscriminately arrested and charged, the defendants plead guilty—as the vast majority do. The trouble with the defense effort is that it is largely misplaced; it is misdirected to a small minority of cases in which legalistic games are made out of real problems.

Another case illustrates how the imbalance in the tribal court sometimes works *against* the defendant. Ostensibly a criminal matter, this case would have been better brought as a civil action—if it was justifiable to bring it at all. The making of civil-criminal distinctions may be viewed as unnecessary in the tribal court context—an "artifice" absent from tribal traditions and sometimes from present practices as well. In this particular case, however, the distinction was not only made but exploited to give the complainants a subsequent (second) civil shot at the defendant.

The defendant is an Indian man in his late twenties or early thirties, who looks like a full-blood but does not speak the tribal language. This is not to his advantage, since the complainants, definitely not full-bloods, have decided to conduct as much of the proceedings as possible in the tribal tongue. The defendant has an amateur translator to help him out, which is, to say the least, unsatisfactory as well as ironical. He has no lawyer or lay advocate.

In the case at hand, the charges against the defendant are illicit cohabitation and nonsupport; the principal complainants are his wife and father-in-law. The defendant is a member of the American Indian Movement (AIM), a group that is generally detested on the reservations but especially by the reservation

---

to put the Indian student back on the team. When the school board refused to respond, at the urging of the lawyer the tribal judge had the members of the board arrested and thrown in the tribal jail. This, of course, created a furor. The dignitaries stayed in jail for eight hours until the tribal council intervened, overruled the tribal judge, and ordered that they be released. The episode has a number of implications, clearly perceived and expressed by the Indian informants. It was evident to them that the tribal judge (if not the whole tribe) had been made to look like a fool, and that his lack of authority had been fully exposed by the overriding action of the tribal council. The action of the Legal Services lawyer—in back of the whole incident—was criticized as being typical of a young-upstart-Legal-Services-type-out-to-make-a-name-for-himself-and-damn-the-consequences. And it was feared that relations between this tribe and the local school board—always important and delicate—might have been well-nigh damaged irreparably as a result of the incident.

establishment.[85] The AIM is particularly unpopular these days on the Navajo Reservation because its recent "occupation" of a major industrial plant on the reservation ultimately resulted in 500 non-AIM Navajos losing their jobs. The current case and charges grow out of this occupation. Normally, the practice of arrest and jailing on charges of illicit cohabitation and nonsupport might be viewed as an instance of the general absence of a conception of probable and sufficient cause on the part of the tribal police, prosecutor, and court. In this particular case, however, it may be more than that; it may also be politics.

The prosecutor, a young Indian layman, is not really effective. But as a matter of psychology, it does not help the defendant to have representation against him when he has none for himself. Concretely, except for a couple of instances, there is not much to put the finger on. The defendant is allowed to cross-examine the witnesses and to tell his own story on the stand rather freely. At only one point does the prosecution object to a question during the defendant's cross-examination of one of the complaining witnesses. When the judge sustains the objection as "irrelevant and immaterial," the defendant hangs his head and says, "No more further questions." But this is only game playing. Rather than being irrelevant, the question simply goes over ground already covered several times (concerning the complainant's own neglect of the children), and the judge is just tired of hearing it. On one other occasion the defendant is constrained in conducting his defense when in beginning his own testimony he indicates that he wants to go back several years in order to "prove his credibility"—meaning his reliability in paying bills and providing support. The judge quietly tells him not to go back so far and to begin with the recent AIM occupation.

On the whole then, the defendant certainly gets his say. This is an important positive aspect of the trial, but it is not enough. For about an hour on the stand, he presents a repetitious mono-

---

[85] The average reservation Indian has few illusions about AIM. Though there are small local chapters of the organization on many reservations, drawing membership from among a few young hotheads (the establishment description), the general consensus is that AIM is basically an outsider—a troublemaking organization. "Nothing but a bunch of urban guerillas" was one of the kinder and more sophisticated characterizations.

logue in which he tries to establish that his own behavior has not been so bad, that his present financial status is no better than his wife's, and that his wife's behavior has been at least as irresponsible, if not worse. It is a story full of common human problems, aspirations, and values: perceived attacks upon his manhood, old-fashioned views about the role of women in society and about the higher standard of moral conduct for women, and so forth. From time to time, when it serves his interest, the defendant pays lip service to the ideals of "sharing" propounded by AIM, or he characterizes certain middle-class values as Indian values. What is really striking is how closely his story resembles so many other stories that can be heard just as frequently off the reservation. One wonders what is "Indian" about this one and why Indian courts and Indian judges are needed to handle it.

All in all, the defendant makes a pretty good case for the proposition that he certainly is at no more fault than the wife and in no better position to shoulder the full burden of support. He also offers a rather implausible rebuttal to the cohabitation charge, stating that he just happened to be sleeping on the same blanket (part of the AIM philosophy of sharing) with another woman when his wife walked in on him at the occupation site. Not being a lawyer or having one, he does not know that this entire cohabitation charge—particularly if based on one incident—is open to attack.

The prosecutor's tactic in cross-examining the defendant is to tediously go over almost every detail, relevant or irrelevant, which has been mentioned in the defendant's rambling monologue. Facts are rehashed about whether the wife's name has indeed "started popping up on the bathroom walls" of local bars, as the defendant has maintained in his "defense." Questions are asked about whether the wife has indeed gotten expensive hairdos every week, whether she really has wasted too much gas driving around in the family pickup trying to get picked up. An incident in which the defendant said he brought coal for the family and was laughed out of the house in ridicule by his wife and in-laws, who insisted that it was just rocks, is lengthily reiterated and subjected to analysis on the order of whether the rocks were in fact coal or just rocks. And the climax of the case comes when the prosecutor pulls out the blanket on which the defendant allegedly did the "illicit cohabiting" with his female corevolutionary:

Prosecutor: [Holding up the blanket] Is this yours?
Defendant: If it's got a cigarette hole in it, it is. [Prosecutor finds cigarette burn.]
Prosecutor: Would you hold this end of the blanket, please?
Defendant: What? Yeah, ok.

With the defendant's help the prosecutor then triumphantly unfurls the blanket, showing that it is not a very big blanket and is therefore "proof beyond a reasonable doubt" (a phrase he throws around continuously) of the defendant's guilt on the charge of cohabitation.

After the final arguments, which contain much trivial repetition, the judge delivers the verdict. He acquits the defendant on the charge of illicit cohabitation, saying it is "all hearsay," which it is not. On the nonsupport charge, the "proof" of which involved a great deal of unsubstantiated hearsay, the judge finds what he calls "substantial evidence," adding a comment to the effect that the defendant has failed to live up to his own philosophizing about the AIM way of life. The sentence is 90 days in jail or a fine of $180 plus a lump sum of $600 to be paid "30 days of the date thereof," as the judge puts it. The defendant just looks defeated and shakes his head. The prosecutor, now talking as plaintiff's lawyer, asks about past damages to the in-laws and future support payments. The judge says this must be brought in a separate civil action (the second crack at the defendant).

Charitable comments about tribal justice—from non-Indians who have an acquaintance with it—are often to the effect that, though the process by which decisions are reached is strange, the decisions are generally "right." With reference to a case like the above, this may be excessively charitable. The next appeal is usually to the good intentions of the judges, as if good intentions were enough. No doubt, most tribal judges are well-intentioned, or at least most of the time. Occasionally, however, as shown above, politics may enter the picture, or self-interest, or social pressure. Combine these with lack of legal knowledge, a handicap in its own right as well as in terms of making judges far more vulnerable to political and social pressures, and one has a system that has difficulty functioning adequately even when it gets beyond the summary.

THEORETICAL PERSPECTIVES[86]

The previous sections have been mainly descriptive, with little theoretical commentary. The purpose of this section is to exam-

---

86. The background reading done for this study also furnishes some comparative perspectives of an anthropological nature. Perhaps the main conclusion that emerges from an examination of other "native," lay, or local justice systems is that comparing their features to the Indian tribal courts is really *not* very apposite. The Indian tribes in this country are fragmented remnants of a past culture almost wholly absorbed by and dependent on the surrounding contemporary culture; the tribal courts are almost wholly duplicative of surrounding nontribal institutions. It does not make much sense to try to compare their situation and characteristics to indigenous, self-sustaining, and self-sufficient systems that reflect, and thus find their legitimacy in, more dominant cultures and larger, less fractionized population groups. Other obstacles to comparison involve jurisdictional differences and distinctions in function and role. For example, it would be hazardous to analogize the workings of the tribal courts which have broad jurisdiction over a "captured" population (the Indian residents of the reservation) with a system such as the Jewish Conciliation Board in Brooklyn whose jurisdiction is consensual and limited to "ethnic" issues, or to the justice of the peace system—as it survives in about two-thirds of the states—whose jurisdiction tends as a practical matter to be far more limited and far less likely to be final than that of the tribal courts. With reference to differences in role and function, it would be inappropriate to make strict comparisons between, for example, the contribution of a lay *jury* to the judicial process and the character of justice as it is dispensed by lay *judges* in tribal courts. Finally, it might be pointed out to those who would insist on comparisons despite the dangers that much of the description of experiences with native/lay justice leaves one with the impression that principles of neutrality and fairness do not thrive in such systems and that the alternative of "professionalism" in the administration of justice, whatever its shortcomings, comes off as very attractive. That impression or judgment may be irrelevant as regards the dominant/indigenous societies where, for one reason or another, there is no history or prospect of professionalism. It is *not* irrelevant to Indians in contemporary U.S. society. Some of the readings upon which the above is based include: Nader, *supra* note 20, especially Nader's own article, Styles of Court Procedure: To Make the Balance, at 69-91; Jane F. Collier, Law and Social Change in Zinacantan (Stanford, Cal.: Stanford University Press, 1973); James Yaffe, So Sue Me! The Story of a Community Court (New York: Saturday Review Press, 1972); Jesse Berman, The Cuban Popular Tribunals, 69 Colum. L. Rev. 1317 (1969); Gordon Smith, Popular Participation in the Administration of Justice in the Soviet Union: Comrades' Courts and the Brezhnev Regime, 49 Ind. L.J. 238 (1974); Note, Modern Roles for Customary Justice: Integration of Civil Procedure in African Courts, 26 Stan. L. Rev. 1123 (1974); Hippler & Conn, note 2 *supra,* including several unpublished manuscripts as well as their Conciliation and Arbitration in the Native Village and the Urban Ghetto, 58 Judicature 228 (1974), and Wedding U.S. Law to Eskimo Tradition, 4 Juris Doctor 41 (April 1974); Note, The Justice of the Peace System under Constitutional Attack—*Gordon v. Justice Court,* 1974 Utah L. Rev. 861; Note, Limiting Judicial Incompetence, and Note, The "Right" to a Neutral and Competent Judge, *supra* note 38; E. Gardner Brownlee, The Revival of the Justice of the Peace in Montana, 58 Judicature 372 (1975); Harry Kalven, Jr., & Hans Zeisel, The American Jury (Boston: Little, Brown & Co., 1966); and Gerhard Casper & Hans Zeisel, Lay Judges in the German Criminal Courts, 1 J. Legal Stud. 135 (1972).

ine some of the theories and assumptions behind the creation and perpetuation of a separate, semiautonomous tribal court system on the reservations. Are these theories and assumptions tenable today?

Indian Justice Versus White Justice

The notion that there are such things as "Indian justice" and "white justice" is too simple and too general to be meaningful. This dichotomy implies a number of equally invalid subdichotomies. Some of the main contrasts are the following:

Indian justice is to white justice as
impartiality is to prejudice
humanism is to legalism
mediation is to adjudication

To talk about white justice is unhelpful, primarily because of the tremendous diversity in justice operations in the United States. How the "system" works varies widely in accordance with conspicuous differences in geography or demography and also in accordance with factors that are less easily identified or understood.

The only brand of white justice that can be meaningfully compared with Indian justice is the rural system operating closest to the reservations, and presumably the one that would be operating on the reservations themselves if it were not for the tribal systems. The stereotype of white justice, based mainly on the experience of urban justice and popularized in the media by observers of the urban scene, has least applicability to rural justice operations.

The term "Indian justice," on the other hand, may be taken to imply that some indigenous, traditional Indian justice arrangement exists. That is not the case. Historically and presently, the justice dispensed in the tribal courts represents nothing more or less than an effort to copy white man's precepts and white man's institutions.

Impartiality Versus Prejudice

One reason given in support of the tribal court system is that Indians would encounter serious prejudice in the outside courts. This consideration leaves one with the curious question of what amount of prejudice justifies what degree of inadequacy in a separate system.

It is true that many Indians believe that they would receive prejudicial treatment in state and county courts. In some areas, this perception is stronger than in others. Interestingly, however, Indians who live under state or county jurisdictions appear less likely to view white prejudice as a problem than those whose experience has been limited to the tribal courts. Whatever their actual experience, most Indian respondents regard the problem of prejudice as a passing one: "Things used to be bad, but they are better now."

In the brief fieldwork for this study, no evidence was uncovered that Indians received adverse treatment in white courts. Whatever the past patterns may have been, anti-Indian prejudice does not appear to be pervasive or systematic in the white courts. The real problem is how to deal with the Indians' negative expectations of white justice.

Politics and rhetoric aside, the Indians' perception of their tribal court system is no more favorable, even on the issue of prejudice. They feel that a considerable amount of prejudice finds its way into the tribal courts. There are countless charges that the tribal judges show favoritism toward council members or their interests, law-enforcement personnel or their friends and relatives, and other "influential groups." Such charges are credible concerning courts in which the judges have insufficient training, stature, support, or experience to be able to insulate themselves from tribal cliques and dissensions.

Humanism Versus Legalism

The rhetoric in support of tribal courts often sets up a contrast between the excessively formal and sterilely technical white courts and the informal and personal tribal courts. As "native institutions," the tribal courts are presumed to be more understanding, more humane than the legalistic white courts. This has not been borne out in observations.

In this study and others,[87] white justice—particularly in rural

---

87. See, e.g., Samuel J. Brakel & Galen R. South, Diversion from the Criminal Process in the Rural Community, 7 Am. Crim. L.Q. 122 (1969).

areas—has been found in many respects to be quite informal and personal. In the state and county courts on or near the reservations, the treatment of both Indians and non-Indians was far from legalistic. Typically, a personalized discretion was exercised, in which the circumstances of the case, the situation of the accused and his or her family, and other particulars were considered in deciding whether to charge, what to charge, how to conduct the proceedings, how to communicate trial rights, whether to accept guilty pleas and waivers of counsel, what standards of decorum to adhere to in trial testimony, and what disposition to make.

For example, in Oklahoma, the county magistrate refused a youth's guilty plea on a narcotics charge, in part because the police evidence was shaky. In North Carolina, the district judge delivered a compromise verdict in a driving-while-intoxicated case against an Indian man who had not been in much trouble before, but he threw the book at an Indian woman who had been a repeat offender of the traffic and narcotics laws. In North Dakota, a state judge questioned individual defendants thoroughly to find out if they had understood their rights before going on with the case, and a county court judge interrupted custody proceedings to talk for 15 minutes privately in chambers to determine what the Indian *child* wanted. In Utah, a defense counsel's thorough cross-examination of the prosecution witnesses in J.P. proceedings before a jury of four brought out the full facts of the arrest and booking process.

In the tribal courts, one finds the surface features of an informal and individualized justice: the tribal judges usually know the people who appear before them; there is little or no case law restricting their discretionary power; except on the Navajo Reservation, court procedure and decorum are quite loose; in the small percentage of contested cases, a wide latitude is permitted with regard to testimony. That, however, is about as far as it goes; underneath there are strong pressures toward a legalistic approach.

First, the tribal judges are insecure. With little formal education, let alone formal legal training, they are at a great disadvantage in dealing with the legal and social complexities of the cases brought before them. This results in a high rate of summary—

typically legalistic—dispositions, in an almost invariable accept-
ance of guilty pleas, and in the standard imposition of fines or
jail sentences. Any other type of processing or disposition is the
exception. It is rare for judges to exercise their discretion imagi-
natively, and it is rare for the individual facts to be developed
fully and subjected to adversary, or in any case detailed, scru-
tiny.

It is also typical for the tribal judges to deal summarily with
the relatively few civil cases that reach the tribal courts. Here,
the lack of knowledge on the part of the judges leads to peculiar
legalisms: the grandiose proclamation against the Housing Authority, for example, or the *ex parte* injunction against the
postal clerk, when neither case involved contesting parties or
contestable issues or resulted in forms of relief that had much
chance of being enforced or even comprehended. In another case
the very judge who issued an officious decree on landownership
dismissed it as meaningless when one of the parties tried to take
it seriously.

In addition to being professionally inadequate, the tribal
judges are politically and socially insecure. They are appointed
and paid by the tribal councils and sometimes removed by the
councils at whim. The reservation tradition is for the councils to
influence or control, often overtly, all phases of reservation business. It may be an encouraging sign that today the judges
recognize and acknowledge the problem of council influence in
judicial affairs and presumably try to deal with it. Still, there are
too many complaints about interference and favoritism to
believe that they deal with it very successfully. One way in
which judges accommodate council pressures is through
legalisms. They are reported to invoke and sustain claims of
sovereign immunity in cases that involve the illegal activity of
council members. Or charges against council members or their
families are dismissed on some other pretext. For example, one
report alleged that when a council member was arrested for
attempted armed robbery on the Navajo Reservation, the judge
dismissed the case at arraignment on the grounds that the police
had not given the defendant a copy of the warrant for arrest in
jail. While political pressures and improprieties are not limited to
the Indian tribal courts, in the tribal courts, from all accounts,

political influence is perceived to be so pervasive and systematic as to constitute the norm.[88]

Being a part of a closed society in which family and clan affiliations exert a powerful influence, tribal judges are very vulnerable to social pressures. People inevitably suspect that social pressures are exerted in judicial matters even when they are not. The judge has few protections against such pressures: the status of his position is not high enough to place him above social squabbles; and he lacks the educational or legal expertise that would compensate for precarious status or enable him to deal with, or effectively disguise a yielding to, improper influence. As a result, the reservation Indians do not perceive the institution of the tribal court to have much, if any, "social" independence.

The problem posed or the suspicion aroused by blood relationship is unavoidable in any close-knit society. Most tribal judges are aware that they should disqualify themselves in cases in which clan or family relation is a factor, but they rarely do. Their reason, which is plausible enough, is that everyone is related to everyone else and that if they took the disqualification option seriously they would be disqualifying themselves all the time. That response, of course, fails to satisfy the parties who come out on the losing end in these situations. It may also be seen as an indictment of the tribal court concept.

Mediation Versus Adjudication

On some imaginary jurisprudential scale, the tribal courts are often put at one mediatory, harmony-seeking extreme and the outside court system at the adjudicatory, accusatory opposite extreme. Comparisons of this kind have their origin in legal-anthropological literature and thought, in which "primitive" (or simply non-Western) justice systems are examined against the background of the contemporary American courts.[89] There is indeed some historical basis for such a contrast in American

---

88. Descriptions of law enforcement in white society at the turn of the twentieth century resemble impressions of the current situation on the reservations. See Mark H. Haller, Historical Roots of Police Behavior: Chicago, 1890-1925, 10 Law & Soc'y Rev. 303 (1976).

89. See Nader, *supra* notes 20 and 86.

Indian traditions and Anglo-American practices. This view, however, does not square with the present-day realities of the Indian
tribal courts or with the expectations of the reservation inhabitants.

The so-called traditional goals of mediation and harmony do
not appear to weigh in the routine thoughts and actions of the
tribal judges, the parties before the tribal courts, or the reservation residents. If one solicited it, most judges and even some
politically oriented residents could engage in rhetoric about such
concepts, but mediation and harmony are not part of their
operational langauge, much less of their practices.

Instead, talk on the subjects of justice and crime took a con-
ventional, unsophisticated, law-and-order form. Judges, council
members, and residents spoke about being tougher on troublemakers. They complained about some defendants getting off
with a slap on the wrist and about the lack of independence on
the part of the courts. On the other hand, defendants complained about high bail and high fines, about the police orienta-
tion of judges, about judges' invariably being harsh and punitive,
and so forth. When one got around to discussing underlying
problems, it was in terms of low salaries for judicial and law-
enforcement personnel, inadequate physical facilities, tribal
politics and factionalism, family jealousies, unemployment, and
alcoholism. In other words, verbalizations about justice on the
reservations were not different from those elsewhere. In fact, the
Indian judges and police often sounded more Anglo than the
Anglos, which is understandable in that they have no model
other than the Anglo system to emulate.

The practices matched the talk: diversionary (noncriminal,
mediatory) handling of criminal matters was, except in a few
systems such as the Navajo's, virtually unheard of. Even the
most marginally criminal cases were typically processed in
straight law-and-order fashion. These included liquor violations,
public drunkenness, vagrancy, nonsupport, illicit cohabitation—
some of which cannot or can no longer be handled as criminal
matters in white courts. Dispositions like probation, working off
the penalty, and delay of conviction upon the accused's being
given a chance to "go straight" were rare in the tribal courts.
Even restitution or the resolution of criminal and civil disputes
in one proceeding—practices in traditional Indian cultures—were

uncommon occurrences. Again with the exception of the Navajo code, the tribal codes made little provision for diversionary solutions, which meant that no encouragement or incentive was given to law-enforcement and judicial personnel to experiment with such possibilities. Even among the Navajo judges, noncriminal dispositions were rare despite tribal code inducements. It is possible that they did not believe in them or that the lack of personnel, programs or physical facilities for "divertible" offenders influenced them. On the other hand, the mere existence of a detoxification center (Standing Rock) or a nursing home (Blackfeet Reservation) did not guarantee that they would be used.

In the tribal courts, the judges rarely attempted to effect reconciliations between disputants or to establish harmony among reservation factions. In general, they made summary dispositions of the cases before reaching the merits. Often, as a result, the parties were left confused and unhappy. When the merits were reached or when all disputants were present, the judges could not prevent acrimonious exchanges from taking place during and after the proceedings. They were often unable to control the parties, and they lacked sufficient authority—real or perceived—to render the proceedings and the outcomes legitimate in the eyes of the litigants. The loser in any court is likely to emerge unhappy, but here the litigants lack of confidence in—and sometimes contempt for—the tribal court process is a different and more serious problem.

One factor that works against a mediatory or reconciliatory role for the court is that the judges are identified with law and order. Many tribal courts have no prosecutor, and the judge himself serves as such; some judges have formerly been tribal police officers; and the reservation people are aware of these facts. The overall picture, then, is that the characteristics of an accusatory system mainly concerned with obtaining convictions, which are usually attributed to the white courts, are more applicable to the tribal courts.

The tendency in the white courts, on the other hand, was not to fully prosecute Indian defendants or hand down jail sentences against them. When interviewed, one district judge even indulged in the popular line that when an Indian "borrowed" a car and "forgot" to return it one could not really call it car theft. Other white law-enforcement officials invoked the alcoholism or different "moral" standards in support of the Indians' lesser accountability and of their own dispositional leniency. Rightly or wrongly, personnel in the white justice system commonly viewed Indians as people with special subcultural attributes and hence with special claims to conciliatory treatment. This is not necessarily always healthy. Resentment about excessive paternalism was found among both whites and Indians outside the law-enforcement system. They singled out the federal system in particular for severe criticism of its treatment (or nontreatment) of major crimes among Indians. Many reasons besides paternalism account for this lack of vigorous federal involvement.[90] One thing is clear, however: the perception of white justice as being excessively accusatory is inaccurate with respect to the treatment of Indian and non-Indian defendants alike.

Cultural Survival Versus Cultural Demise

Persons who favor the continued operation of the tribal courts often associate the survival of the courts with the survival of tribal culture in general, and vice-versa. The demise of the courts, they say, would spell the demise of Indian culture. While it appears to be logical and has an immediate appeal, this either-or, all-or-nothing stance should be considered more closely.

It is implied that if one does not support one tribal institution one is anti-Indian, that if one does not recognize a total political-cultural autonomy for the Indians one must favor a total melting-pot assimilation. All claims of separate autonomy are regarded as natural; any movement toward integration is regarded as imposed and artificial. Such an extreme position is not helpful in discussing Indian affairs and problems in general or in assessing the workability of the tribal courts.

Whatever historical or moral arguments one may muster to the contrary, whatever ancient doctrines of "residual" sovereignty[91] or present-day claims to white reparations may exist, it

---

90. Other reasons include evidentiary problems caused by noncooperation of witnesses; noncooperation and/or lack of skill of tribal officials; lack of both federal and tribal investigative manpower; distance; jury reluctance to convict; competing prosecutorial priorities; and so forth.

91. See note 7 *supra*.

appears anomalous in the latter part of the twentieth century that one small ethnic group should be separated from the judicial system that extends to all other citizens of the United States. The burden of persuasion for separatist ideas should fall on the proponents of separatism. In the case for separate tribal courts, instead of advancing the usual political and mystical arguments, proponents should show that the courts have concrete operational advantages.

The present performance of the tribal courts can hardly be said to indicate the vitality of Indian tribal culture. Terminating their operation does not mean the end of Indian culture, realistically defined. Finally, in contrast with tribal leaders or spokesmen, the average reservation resident has little interest in seeing the tribal court system maintained or expanded.

Indian Courts Versus Indian Culture

In both conception and operation, the tribal courts are little more than pale copies of the white system. All remedies to their operational problems are directed toward making them better copies. This leaves only "localism" as a justification for their existence—that is, the desire for and convenience of locally controlled institutions. Local control, however, must be exercised responsibly: there must be mechanisms to check abuse of power and to promote optimum use of talent. In my view, official authority would be best utilized and personal power on the reservations would be best checked within the normal integrated setting of, and with the mechanisms available under, state and county jurisdiction. In twentieth-century America, the integrated approach is the only realistic and the only acceptable approach (for Indians as well as non-Indians). Integration into the larger judicial system does not necessarily threaten the preservation of the elements of Indian culture that are capable of being preserved or the revival of those that are worthy of being revived any more than the perpetuation of a dependent and often inauthentic tribalism would guarantee them.

Even the most favored of the tribal courts are burdened by inexperienced and unprofessional judges, administrative and procedural irregularity, substantively inadequate fact finding, and insufficient exploration of the legal content or social implications of cases. To these, one must add the problems of perceived partiality toward particular political or social factions and, in the less favored courts, perhaps the reality of discrimination, in addition, or the outright abdication of juridical responsibilities. Even on the more "progressive" reservations, public confidence in the tribal courts is at best meager. Efforts to improve the courts are toward making them more like white courts or, worse, like a stereotype of white courts. White academics and professionals provide training sessions for Indian judges; often inexperienced white lawyers and advisors expand or revise the tribal codes; Congress passes an Indian Bill of Rights that is modeled on the United States Constitution; the federal courts are acquiring a broader jurisdiction in Indian criminal affairs; white judges or lawyers are being hired to sit on the "tribal courts"; Indian judges begin to wear black robes; courtrooms are built or remodeled to resemble "real" (i.e., white) courts; and so on. What relation do these practices have to Indian tribal culture?

It requires no great leap of logic to arrive at the view that all this is a roundabout way of achieving what can be achieved more directly through the "solution" of integration. That is not to say that extending state and county jurisdiction to the reservations would be without trauma or without the need for special formulas to assure Indian participation and representation; many Indians have negative perceptions of white justice; white officials are entrenched in most law-enforcement positions; and the Indians are at a great educational disadvantage. Nevertheless, integration is the only approach with real promise: it is inevitable in the long run, and it is not necessarily out of tune with the current trends (as opposed to the rhetoric) in Indian life and culture. The model of Indian justice for the 1970s and the future is not the Dakota, Montana, or even the Arizona (Navajo) one, but rather the Oklahoma model.

All steps taken to preserve the tribal courts or the reservation system can only be rearguard actions. The reservations, with their courts and other institutions, are destined to disappear in time. The only question is, When? The true motivations behind, and justification for, Indian separatism are psychological. As in the black movement in this country, separatist rhetoric may be useful in restoring a sense of personal (or "cultural," if one insists) identity and worth to the members of an ethnic minority that has a history of being suppressed, exploited, and kept dependent. That is its total role. To recognize that does not mean that one should become an accomplice in the creation or perpetuation of artificial, separatist institutions. The time appears to be ripe to expose the temporary, psychological purposes of these institutions and to inform the Indians of more permanent, functional alternatives. It is time to acknowledge that Indian reservations do not preserve Indian culture. They are little more than depressed areas for marginal and dependent societies of Indians, whites, and mixed-bloods. They are sociological nurseries to which those who find life difficult outside can always return, places of more or less voluntary detention for the ones who have never left, zoos for white tourists, and laboratories for academics. Tribal courts do not exemplify an Indian culture worth preserving; they are imitations of white institutions, beset by aggravated versions of the problems of white institutions and characterized in part by the preservation in power of a few individuals whose own "Indianness" and whose concern for the Indian people are often suspect.

Indian Courts Versus the Indian People

It is difficult to ascertain what the Indian people want.[92] Many of them are quite cynical about reservation life and reservation institutions, including the tribal courts. On the other hand, they are ignorant of or equally cynical about, if not fearful of, the alternatives. The Indians who have had some experience in the outside world and with white institutions usually express mixed feelings about their experiences. The current emphasis on "Indianness" and autonomy only complicates the picture for them. Those who have had no experience with white institutions also are influenced by the prevailing separatist rhetoric.

Few would argue the point that the reservation people should be left to choose for themselves. If they are to choose, however, they must be informed of the facts; and the misconceptions about the differences between Indian and non-Indian life and practices must be dispelled.

---

92. It is clear that the Indian "leadership" wants retrocession. What the average reservation residents want is a different matter, but the communication power of the leaders makes it likely that they will drift toward separatist views as well.

For example, the ideas that tribal institutions and courts are genuinely Indian, that they benefit the Indian people, and that Indians unanimously endorse and support them are all largely mythical. Equally groundless is the idea that contemporary non-tribal institutions are unsuitable for Indians, although with sufficient propaganda it could become a self-fulfilling prophecy. Sometimes persons who are willing to acknowledge the systemic problems of tribal existence and tribal institutions and the dissatisfaction of Indian individuals with them are apt to put the issue in terms of the need to sustain "tribal rights" over "individual rights" in the long-term interest of Indian individuals. The argument is unconvincing in view of the almost certain disappearance of tribalism and separatism in the long term.

Efforts to improve the tribal courts with robes, money, new courtrooms, and more training programs are only band-aid measures, as are efforts to improve reservation conditions with more welfare money, food stamps, motels, resorts, oil and gas leases, and Washington, D.C., lawyers. The alternative of integrating the tribal judicial system with state and county institutions has many advantages. By definition, it would eliminate the Kafkaesque confusion among tribal, state, and federal courts and other agencies. At the same time, the Indian people would be no less free to be "Indian," "rural," "traditional," or "bound to the land or community" or to choose whatever life-style and values they may want. By the same token, the many Indians who want to embark on ("acculturated") professional careers would probably have a better chance to succeed and a better setting in which to use their professional skills. Today, Indians who want professional careers often fail at both realizing their ambitions and maintaining a satisfactory contact with the reservation.

CONCLUSIONS AND RECOMMENDATIONS

The tribal courts do not work well, and necessary improvements would require much time and involve many difficulties. To perpetuate them at all runs counter to the evolutionary trends in the Indians' relation to the dominant culture in this country. Therefore, it would be more realistic to abandon the system altogether and to deal with Indian civil and criminal problems in the regular county and state court systems. Existing integrated arrangements appear to work well enough. Integrated justice systems, however, could be improved by the employment of Indians in nonprofessional, advisory capacities in the whole range of law-enforcement and justice-administration posts until such time that more than the present few could participate fully as professional equals. There is no historical basis for the fear that putting the Indian people under the regular justice systems will hasten the demise of their culture and traditions.

Integration is especially urgent for the smaller, less-organized tribes or reservations, where the chances are slim that they will ever have sufficient human or economic resources to achieve an adequate standard of justice and government.

It is likely that many tribes will initially reject any recommendation of integration, especially the larger tribes, like the Navajo, in which the ethos of autonomy and sovereignty has had some substantiation in fact.[93] In view of this probable rejection, recommendations will follow for improving those tribal courts that will continue in operation.

Any measure taken to improve existing tribal court operations could have troublesome repercussions and ramifications: it would be easy to upset the already precarious balance of a tribal court system or to further impair one that is already unbalanced. Consider, as one example, the possible impact of a recommendation that professional defense lawyers be regularly brought into the tribal courts. The potential for disruption of the tribal court process if such a recommendation were implemented could in itself be construed as an argument in favor of total change, that is, in favor of turning to the professionalized and better-balanced state and county systems.

Professional Personnel

The primary need of the tribal justice systems is for judges and law-enforcement personnel with training and experience. How can they be acquired? In some ways, the reservation setting is not conducive to the obtaining of education or of professional experience. Only today for the first time are a significant num-

---

93. Even so, I believe that state and county jurisdiction (integration) is the proper, and ultimately the only, solution for the major tribes as well.

ber of reservation people receiving formal higher education, including training in law schools. These young people—in their early twenties—usually come from the more acculturated (often mixed-blood) families, and they receive their training outside the reservations. One may question whether they will be inclined to return to the reservations permanently. Those who do choose to come back will not yet have the professional or social experience that would equip them to assume important decision-making functions. They will not be ready for the role of tribal judges. On the other hand, the older reservation people, from whose ranks the present tribal judges are generally chosen, have a better acquaintance with reservation life and personalities and political and social realities; but with very little formal education of any kind, they are difficult to train in the law.

The existing training programs have an element of hopelessness about them, and one cannot be more optimistic about new ones. First, there is a scarcity of good teachers who both understand the law and are able to communicate their knowledge to such an unusual student group. The students themselves have complicated objectives, a limited training time, and because of reservation policies and politics, a high dropout rate.

On the operational level, several remedial steps merit consideration. At present, the workings of the tribal courts are characterized by inadequate fact finding and lack of open contest, and a forced "simplification" in the cases brought exists simultaneously with an overcriminalization of issues that are essentially noncriminal. The suggested remedies, which are not mutually exclusive, pose problems: First, can they be achieved at all? Second, will they produce repercussions that will nullify the gains?

Legal Representation

Legal representation could be made available, especially at the arraignment or preliminary hearing and for advice before the initiation of litigation. But *how* can it be made available? Who will pay for it? Should it be provided by professional attorneys or Indian lay advocates? The first two questions belong to the issue of bringing legal services to the poor and to the geographically isolated, in general, and need not be dealt with separately at this point.[94] The third question is relevant here.

For defendants charged with crimes, the advantages of having access to professional counsel are obvious. For "the system," however, professional counsel may be disadvantageous. If it is to the benefit of his client, a professional lawyer will be competent at bringing out the full facts and their legal and social implications. If not, he will try to terminate the inquiry early by way of certain permitted procedural or substantive methods; and in the inexpert and unbalanced tribal court, he is almost sure to succeed. Thus, the client may receive an immediate benefit, but this exploitation of the inadequacies of the tribal court will not serve the broader interest of promoting justice on the reservation.

In theory, lay advocates have a less disruptive effect in the tribal courts. They are, in addition, said to be more accessible to the clients. In practice, these expectations do not always hold.

The availability of lay advocates is easily exaggerated. On some reservations, there are none. On one reservation with thousands of cases per year, there are only one or two advocates. Even on a reservation with a relatively large and well-organized lay-advocate system, many parties go unrepresented at the crucial preliminary or arraignment stages, where most dispositional determinations occur.

In some courts, lay advocates, having learned a few tricks of the lawyer's trade, assume a disruptive, unbalancing stance. For example, almost every charge and complaint can be attacked for legal insufficiency, owing to the nonprofessionalism of the police and prosecutors, and such tactics will succeed if the judges are unable or unwilling to maintain balance and control in their courts.

One solution is to have professional lawyers who are not limited by a one-to-one adversary perspective. But where are they to be found? How are they to be identified? Further, can a nonadversarial role be played in the tribal courts or anywhere else?

---

94. For a look at the general issue of legal services to the poor, see Samuel J. Brakel, Judicare: Public Funds, Private Lawyers, and Poor People (Chicago: American Bar Foundation, 1974).

Balancing of the System

Another solution might be to balance the system by having professional expertise for the bench, the prosecutor, and both parties. The prospects of achieving this are remote. It would take a long time for the local Indian people to produce lawyers who are able and willing to fill these posts. On the other hand, if imported white lawyers assume these functions, the tribal courts will cease to exist except in name.

Increased and better representation of litigants, or increased professionalism generally, may overburden the courts and make them unable to handle the large caseloads. There are several possible solutions.

Obtaining of Facts

Apart from increasing their number, judges could be trained to assume the basic responsibility of obtaining as many facts as possible relating to the offense, offender, dispute, or parties before going on with the judicial processing (even if this is usually only a matter of accepting a guilty plea). At present, tribal judges do not see this as a part of their role, and there is no one else to do it either. If an adequate preliminary inquiry were made, probably many cases could be dismissed and others handled through noncriminal dispositions or out of court, thus offsetting the burdens imposed by fuller initial inquiries.

Screening of Cases

Similarly, before making formal arrests and charges, the police and the prosecutors should be trained to screen out cases that could be handled informally or dropped altogether. At present, they dump everything on the tribal court. One big question is, Can the tribal policemen and prosecutors be trained to take sound discretionary action based on preliminary inquiries? Whatever the answer, it is clear that this approach has no place in existing training programs. One of the prime contributing factors to the overall problem of indiscriminate, summary justice on the reservations is the fact that every harmless alcoholic, every husband whose wife has a domestic complaint, and every minor traffic violator is hauled before the tribal court in the same way as the genuinely violent or deviant offender.

Counteraction of Political and Social Pressures

Tribal judges should be made less vulnerable to political and social pressures. Since there is no tradition of professionalism to shield them from these pressures, direct methods of protection should be considered: (a) better ways should be found for selecting judges; (b) judges should be given secure tenure; (c) judges should be made immune from council influence; and (d) disqualification procedures should be established to cover cases in which judges are open to clan or family influence or other social pressures. These measures may not be easy to implement.

Experience indicates that selection of judges by the tribal council opens the way for selection of individuals who can be manipulated and for interference with ongoing court operations. Popular elections, on the other hand, raise the specter of popularity contests, with judicial candidates behaving in such a way as to win or retain votes. While these potential problems apply to the selection of judges anywhere, they are accentuated in the closed societies of the reservations, where there are no traditions of separation of powers in government or of judicial professionalism in particular.

Providing secure tenure for judges must be counterbalanced, of course, by providing for their removal under compelling circumstances. Any removal apparatus, however carefully circumscribed, opens the way for political abuse. On the reservations, the present consensus is that the appointment of judges and the decisions regarding their tenure are based entirely on politics. It is encouraging that some reservations are adopting laws and rules designed to eliminate such abuses.

To guard against political and social pressures being brought to bear upon ongoing court operations, tribal codes and council regulations should explicitly spell out procedures to be used to detect such influence and to protest against it.

The more radical proposal of having judges from neighboring reservations replace the local judges in politically or socially sensitive cases has been advanced on occasion. The problem then becomes, Who will identify such cases? Proposals to hire non-local Indian judges for all cases do not appear to take into account the fact that in such a permanent relationship the nonlocal judge would soon become subject to many of the same pressures that face local judges, as well as some additional ones.

A judge from a different tribe or band is likely to be strongly resented by reservation people, who often find it difficult enough to tolerate authority that is exercised by individuals from different families, clans, or towns within the same reservation. The main "advantage" of lay justice is that of being judged by one's own, an objective that would be destroyed by hiring lay judges from other reservations. To hire local white attorneys to sit on the tribal courts might be more tolerable; some of the mystique of localism would be preserved and at the same time the average reservation resident would value the professionalism.

Sometimes, too, exchanging tribal judges is seen as a means to make appeals meaningful. Currently, on the rare occasion when the appellate process is invoked, the results are predictable; the same or practically the same people that hear the initial case will hear the appeal. Even in the best tribal appellate systems, the granting and resolution of appeals is flawed to the extent that it is the sole province of the chief justice. Provided that it is feasible in terms of time, money, and willingness on the part of the courts—all of which is doubtful—having judges from other reservations hear appeals might make the appellate process more "legitimate." Alternatively, state or county judges or local lawyers could be asked to serve as appellate judges. It is possible that such a limited non-Indian involvement would be acceptable even to those strongly concerned about the "Indianness" of the courts.

The handling of the major crimes committed on the reservations in the federal courts has presented major problems: (a) the distances involved make it difficult for federal officials to conduct investigations or to obtain cooperation from witnesses; (b) the federal prosecutors often have other priorities; (c) the off-reservation juries are either overly sympathetic or unconcerned; and (d) when the federal courts attempt to refer cases to the tribal courts, the tribal officials are often not responsive. The overall result has been a serious lack of enforcement. If the jurisdiction over major crimes were turned over to local state or county authorities, most of these difficulties would probably be solved or at least mitigated. One can expect considerable Indian opposition to this proposal, however.

A more palatable alternative, for the Indians, may be to have major crimes handled in the tribal courts with imported professional judges and imported lawyers for both sides. In effect, this would mean nontribal or non-Indian control over the handling of major criminal cases, but the location would be convenient for the victims, defendants, witnesses, and Indian juries. As currently constituted and operating, the tribal courts and tribal personnel are not equipped to handle major crimes.

Salaries, Facilities, Equipment

The adjustment of judicial salaries to levels competitive within the reservation environment is desirable, but large increases designed to be competitive with the outside world do not seem justified so long as the courts essentially do not want to attract outsiders. New physical facilities and equipment are not top-priority items. Should money nonetheless be made available for construction and staffing, the following priorities might be observed.

First, on the reservations where they are nonexistent or inadequate, facilities and staff should be provided for the treatment of the many alcoholics who are routinely routed through the tribal criminal system. Hospitals and detoxification centers will not guarantee wise court decisions or solve the problem of alcoholism on the reservations, but they will help facilitate more appropriate and humane handling.

Second, juvenile offenders should have separate detention and treatment facilities. On most reservations, juveniles and adults are housed in the same jails, appear in the same courts, and participate in the same, if any, treatment programs.

Third, if possible, tribal judges and other court and enforcement personnel should be paid more. At present, tribal judges usually earn $10,000 or less per year; even by reservation standards, this salary is too low to be competitive with tribal or BIA jobs of comparable status or responsibility. As a result, judges have been resigning to take better-paying jobs; the morale of those who stay has remained low; and fewer reservation people are being attracted to judicial service. As a minimum, judicial pay should be made competitive with comparable reservation positions.

Construction or improvement of tribal court facilities, police headquarters, prosecutor's offices, jails, and so forth, while not undesirable, are items that merit attention only after the higher priorities have been satisfied. Compared with standard living conditions among the reservation people, the existing facilities are not bad. Modern buildings and plush offices may cause resentment among a population that is already too familiar with self-serving tribal authorities, and they would have little effect on the effort to improve tribal justice.

appendix

THE FORT TOTTEN SYSTEM[95]

The Devils Lake (Fort Totten) Sioux Reservation, in terms of topography and vegetation, is unlike the prevailing Dakota landscape and certainly unlike the areas in which Indian reservations are usually found. It is a comparatively small reservation, bounded on the north by a complex of lakes collectively called Devils Lake and on the south by the uncertain course of the Sheyenne River. In between, forming the body of the reservation, are wooded hills—not very high but short and choppy, not majestically wooded exactly but quite unlike the mainly treeless flats to slight but long undulations that characterize the landscape for miles and miles around. Just off the reservation on the northern side of the lake area is the white town of Devils Lake, which has about 7,000 people, a sizeable place for this sparsely populated part of the country. Fort Totten is the main town on the reservation and houses a large share of its approximately 1,500-2,000 residents. Devils Lake has a small airport whose weather station from time to time in the winter months records the lowest temperatures in the 48 contiguous states.

There appears to be particularly little opportunity or hope for development and employment on the Fort Totten Reservation. The Devils Lake complex attracts a few tourists and some moneyed local (white) people,

---

95. Technically, the Fort Totten situation is unique in that the state of North Dakota has explicit concurrent jurisdiction with the tribal court over Indian offenses. During my fieldwork, I did not hear any commentary on or observe any operational consequences of this situation. It explains, however, why the white visiting judge at Fort Totten is indeed a judge rather than simply a local attorney.

and ventures to stimulate more of the same are being planned; but since little development is occurring on the reservation side of the water, there will not be much economic benefit to the tribe. The lakes are used for some fishing for sport by the Indians; for the rest, their main impact seems to be that from time to time the waters flood the road to the town of Devils Lake and threaten to cut off the reservation from "civilization."

The tribal court is located in a one-story prefab law-and-order building, alongside the tribal police offices and jail. Physical facilities and personnel are minimal. There is a chief judge and associate judge but no prosecutor, defense mechanism, probation or juvenile department, or any of the other accessories of a court system. Two Indian women serve as combination court clerk-secretary-receptionists. Records and recordings of proceedings are primitive or lacking. There has been some office and courtroom renovation recently, but on the whole the accommodations remain makeshift and cramped. The judges rely heavily, if not exclusively, on a white visiting judge for contested cases, although this does not mean that the Indian judges have altogether removed themselves from decision making. Many arraignments after all call for difficult and definitive determinations. White social workers from Devils Lake play a role in domestic cases tried before the white judge. (This judge, in contrast with the visiting judge at Standing Rock, who was a private practitioner, is also a judge of the district courts of North Dakota.)[96] Extreme informality characterizes Fort Totten tribal justice when the Indian judges are in charge. (One will recall that the Navajo judges were very formal.)

In the absence of statistical information, one must rely exclusively on descriptive material for a picture of the operations of the Fort Totten court.

A disinclination toward responsible decision making seems to characterize the operations of the tribal court and is facilitated by the availability of the visiting judge and the fragmentary and incomplete shape of the tribal code. The atmosphere of informality and loose responsibility in the Fort Totten court produces an impression (also, but more faintly, derived from experiences on other reservations) that the tribal judges are only playing at being judges. If it is indeed a game, the stakes are far too high from the defendants' point of view as well as from the standpoint of the social well-being of the whole reservation.

The chief judge's knowledge of the content of the code and his general grasp of the law and of its role are limited. This is easily understandable, given his lack of experience and training. Indeed, at our initial meeting, he was found reading the code—"trying to familiarize myself," as he put it. At

---

96. See *supra* note 95.

that time he had been in office for only two weeks. At the time of my second visit one year later, it appeared that the familiarity he had gained was primarily with the flexibility inherent in a jurisdiction in which several systems of law are concurrently applicable. An example follows.

At one point during the course of a long and relatively inactive day, an Indian man walks into the judge's office. There is no display of officious formality here: the two men talk together like the old friends that they are. The problem is that the visitor has brought with him a traffic ticket from the highway patrol charging him with driving without a muffler. In effect, he has come in for an "advance verdict," and the judge complies by telling him that he will "throw it out, because it's not covered in the code."

The noncoverage "verdict," however, is not "legitimate." First, there is enough in the tribal code to cover the muffler violation ("required equipment," "unsafe conditions," etc.) Moreover, even without specifically applicable language in the tribal code, the general provision to the effect that the code is to be supplemented with relevant state law when necessary would be sufficient to cover the violation. Whatever the chief judge's limitations in legal knowledge and experience, he is not unaware of these facts. In a conversation immediately preceding the muffler incident, he had commented on how "broad" the tribal code was: "It doesn't have much in it, but you can do just about anything with it." From there, he had gone on to make reference to using the applicable state law in cases where the code was not broad (or specific) enough.

Other evidence of the judge's attitude to the law and his job, as well as deeper difficulties affecting Fort Totten tribal justice, is readily detectable. Regarding a Devils Lake drug case that was thrown out of the county court because of "illegal police behavior," the judge commented that the police should have claimed they were making a "citizen's arrest." His casual descriptions of the juvenile problems rampant on the Fort Totten Reservation, including drinking, pot smoking, and glue sniffing, and comments on the *political* impossibility of doing anything about them also struck me as unfortunate. Stories of strained relations between the tribal court and BIA officials and between the court and white lawyers and state and county officials in neighboring Devils Lake (of which the muffler case appears to be one specific indication) did not help to give a more favorable impression.

A description of case proceedings confirms the problems. Five arraignments are held one afternoon, starting at 2:00. Before the proceedings begin, the judge sifts through a large stack of warrants, subpoenas, and summonses, which, he says, the police have failed to serve. "It happens all the time," he adds, apparently resigning himself to it. Next, a custody hearing that was originally scheduled for this time slot is called off because the "social studies" (the report of the social worker) are not ready. Then the five arraignees, a sad-looking lot, are brought in; none are older than their early twenties.

1) The first case concerns an escape from the reservation jail—a frequent occurrence on each reservation visited. It is the second escape for this particular accused. He mechanically pleads guilty and receives an additional three-month sentence.

2) The second case is a drunken-driving charge. When it turns out that the wrong defendant is sitting in court, the judge gets off the bench and walks over to the police department himself to get the right man, shaking his head in dismay while doing so. A plea of guilty follows, and the disposition is a $30 fine plus a few days to come up with the money. This is rather lenient.

3) Next is a reckless-driving case. The resolution is routine—guilty plea and fine—except that the judge is unable to find the relevant tribal code provision.

4) Assault and battery, immediate plea of guilty, and $75 fine plus six months' probation is the sequence for the fourth case.

5) The last "arraignment," however, throws the court into a tizzy. The charge is contributing to the delinquency of a minor, but with that all certainty ends. The defendant seems to think he is appealing an earlier conviction on this charge by the associate judge, whereas the present chief judge is treating it as an initial arraignment. The defendant makes an effort to explain that he has already served part of a six-month sentence, then pleads not guilty; he is finally taken back to the jail while the judge tries to figure out what is going on.

The mention of appeal, in the meantime, has set off a reaction among the other four defendants. Now the first accused (jail escape), speaking from the back of the courtroom where he is still sitting, says that he wants to appeal too. The judge's response is that it is too late to appeal the first escape conviction but that it is all right for the most recent one, an offense to which the accused pleaded guilty 10 minutes earlier. What the grounds might be is not indicated.

Meanwhile, the young Indian who pleaded guilty to reckless driving also has a change of heart. Although his sentence is only a fine, he is afraid he will lose his job, so he wants to "appeal." The judge, who by now appears to have lost control of the courtroom, gives in; and something amounting to either a change in plea or an appeal on the guilty plea is entered.

Later, the judge voices his displeasure at what transpired in the courtroom. "Some of these guys are getting pretty smart," he says, echoing a view expressed by tribal judges on other reservations, namely, that it is somehow subversive and disruptive for Indians to begin to see and assert rights, hire lawyers, and so forth. The demand for appeals is not an immediate or serious threat. Because the appellate role is played by the same judges who do trial work, with the exception of the judge who handled the original case, affirmation is almost invariably the rule, as the chief judge freely admits. (On Standing Rock, the chief judge went one step further in volunteering the view that the role of the appeals court was to "support" the trial judges. "We have to stand together," he added.)

The following day, the white district judge comes in to sit and render judgment in the tribal court. The difference made by legal training and experience, and the sense of authority that comes with them, become abundantly apparent.

Among the cases handled by the state judge are three debtor-creditor disputes. There are no attorneys involved on either side. In each case the plaintiff is the white operator of a small reservation grocery store who is suing some of his Indian customers for failure to pay bills. He makes his own case in a brief statement, supported by copies of the unpaid bills, signed by the debtors, which have accumulated unpaid over the period of about one year.

 In the first case, the defendant is a middle-aged woman. The judge gives her the opportunity to examine the bills and her signatures. She claims that a couple of slips were not signed by her or by any members of her family and hence that she is not responsible for them. Otherwise she does not disclaim her liability. The judge, perhaps as a gesture of compromise, buys this partial defense, particularly since there is no strong comeback from the creditor. He thus subtracts the amount on the dubious slips from the $307 total originally claimed and finds for the creditor to the amount of $264. The defendant is to pay this at a rate of $10 per month. Confronted with the final, authoritative disposition, the woman becomes furious. She now charges that the grocer has probably altered some of the figures on the slips and starts hollering to the audience about whites "screwing us poor Indians." She also demands an appeal to an "all-Indian jury." The judge just quietly lets her go on for a while without responding. Pretty soon, the woman quiets down herself, mumbling something to the effect that, even if resentfully, she will probably comply with the court's judgment.

 In the second case, the debtor is a man in his thirties whose "defense" is that he has had unforeseen financial difficulties, which are now behind him. He promises to begin payment immediately. The grocer thinks this is good enough and indicates it to the judge. The agreement is recorded, and the case is closed.

The third case revives the atmosphere of hostility between creditor and debtor. The defendants are a young couple who have no real defense. Instead, they complain that the grocer's prices are too high, maintain that they paid some of their debts off more than a year ago, and ask why the grocer should now be so quick to take them to court. The judge permits a brief acrimonious exchange between the disputants, then ends it by order-ing the defendants to pay off the debt at the apparently formula rate of $10 per month. While still grumbling and somewhat bitter, the defendants accept this verdict.

The impression received from these cases is very favorable on one level: one might almost contend that this is what justice in relatively minor disputes should look like—informal, yet authoritative; no wasted motion or procedure, yet everyone has his or her say, even to the point of being allowed to let off some steam.

Underneath, however, there is the problem of the Indians' perception, exhibited most strongly by the woman in the first case, of being "done in" by the white world. The white judge reinforces that view, no matter how fairly and equitably the proceedings are conducted. The losing party will always look behind the merits; it is almost unavoidable that Indian defen-dants who are accused and judged by whites will consider themselves vic-timized. In fact, that feeling appears to pervade much of reservation life. The Indian judges are not entirely clear of the charge of victimizing poor Indians either; they get accused of selling out to the white world, whereas the white judge has nothing to sell to begin with.

Perhaps to counteract the kind of accusation mentioned above, the Indian judges, on Fort Totten and elsewhere, sometimes seem to work to undermine the authority of the white judge. For example, after the debtor-creditor proceedings are over, the chief judge at Fort Totten gives vent to his feeling that justice may not have been done because the grocer marks up his prices and therefore ought to suffer the consequences. He feels that the man's credit policies are such that his entitlement to the debts incurred by his customers should somehow be diminished. Whatever its propriety, this opinion is contradicted by testimony given during the proceedings which indicated that the grocer was certainly not grossly irre-sponsible in his credit policies. Also, it would seem that the economic realities of running a small store on the reservation justify some markup in prices over those of the large chain stores in the neighboring white towns.

The underlying problem is that, by and large, the reservation people, including the tribal judges, lead "white men's" lives, economically marginal lives perhaps, but white men's lives nonetheless, with white men's problems and aspirations; but they are poorly equipped in terms of upbringing, experience, education, and resources for advice or help to deal with this life-style. The consequences of this on judicial functioning are various: Some Indian judges take an excessive "law-and-order" or moralistic stance; others react with defensiveness, a false "cultural" assertiveness, which ranges from the amusing to the destructive. Lack of legal and political knowledge or of confidence only compounds the problem. For example, during a break in the proceedings conducted by the white judge in the Fort

Totten court, the associate tribal judge came in from an adjoining office waving an "injunction" that he had just prepared against the regional Housing Authority. It purported to stop the Housing Authority from building on the reservation until the following requirements were met: that the construction be better; that no homes be built for whites; that full-bloods have first pickings; and a number of other strange provisos. All this, stated in convoluted pseudolegalese (reminiscent of the land-sale "authorization" on Standing Rock), was offered without any indication of who the aggrieved were, who the intended beneficiaries of the injunction would be, what the complaints or problems were, what prompted the "resolution" of the problems, or anything. When asked what he thought of it and what he would "do about it," the white judge only smiled benevolently and noncommitally.

The fact remains, however, that often the visiting white judge is the only authority respected by the common Indian people; despite their occasional comments to the contrary and their bitterness when they come out on the losing side in court, the people usually exhibit a genuine awe of formal education and formal experience. In an interview, a white judge (from a reservation that was not studied in depth) claimed that many times Indian litigants had *requested* to be tried before him in the tribal court rather than go before one of the Indian judges, while only once in his two and one-half years of experience had the opposite request been made. But this sort of evidence does not sit well with the tribal politicians who see it as a cultural affront, or with the judges, who see it as a personal and professional affront. In extreme instances, according to reports, the result is that individual decisions by the visiting white judges are simply vitiated by "appeals" to the tribal council or tribal judges. Subtler actions to the same effect include "suspending" the penalties imposed by white judges or not implementing them because of "clerical errors." Meanwhile, general tribal policies are in the direction of a tacit phasing out, if not an explicit termination, of the white judges' role in the reservation courts.(97)

---

(97) Because of Indian opposition—mainly reservation establishment opposition—the visiting white judge system, then, cannot be a solution to the tribal court problems. This is regrettable, because observations seemed to show that the tribal court worked best that way, despite the fact that losing litigants could find some special excuse for resentment in the notion that they had been "done in" by a white judge. If "political" opposition can be overcome, the best visiting judge system will be one that employs not just local lawyers but lawyers who are actually county or district judges or who have had prior judicial experience. What should be avoided is the use of inexperienced young white lawyers (or law students, as was the temporary situation on one reservation). Not just any legally trained person will do; the individual involved in the sensitive task of being judge in the tribal court must also have the maturity and authority that come with experience and general community standing.

THE UINTAH AND OURAY SYSTEM

The Uintah and Ouray Ute Indian Reservation is located in Utah, southeast of Salt Lake City on the other side of the Wasatch Mountain Range. It occupies portions of a broad valley the northern edge of which is formed by the high Uinta Mountains, a large "primitive area" and, as a point of interest, the only major mountain range in the United States running from east to west (as opposed to essentially north-south). The valley slopes ever downward to the east, becoming progressively drier as it approaches the Green River and the western border of Colorado. The reservation stops short of reaching the man-made boundary and instead takes an abrupt southward turn at the natural one, the Green River, which provides rough guidelines for the shape and direction of this southern strip of reservation land.

Much of the Uintah and Ouray Reservation is quite broken up; within the "boundaries" of the reservation, large land areas are owned by whites, and several towns—for example, Roosevelt and Duchesne—are essentially white. The main Indian settlements are *Fort* Duchesne—as distinguished from just plain Duchesne—and White Rocks, some 30-40 miles east of Duchesne and about 150 miles southeast of Salt Lake City. Basically, the land is rocky and dry—semidesert to real desert; but irrigation in the river valleys permits limited farming, and some natural vegetation in the valleys and on the mountain slopes allows a small amount of grazing. Some tourism and hunting and fishing are possible and are in fact beginning to be exploited in the mountain and river-canyon lands. Timber is a resource at the northern fringes of the reservation on the foothills of the Uinta Mountains. The biggest economic boon to the Utes, however, is the arid southern strip—which contains virtually no vegetation, neither brush nor tree, only some wild horses, but which has significant subsurface oil and gas reserves. These reserves, which have been leased out by the Utes, produce a considerable income for individuals and for the tribe. While distribution of this income is unequal, few Utes appear to be destitute, and as a general matter, there certainly is money on the reservation.

The total Indian population of the reservation stands at slightly below 2,000.[98] Some 1,300-1,400 of these are officially listed as full-bloods, and about 300-400 are mixed. Only the full-bloods are full, "enrolled" tribal members; the mixed-bloods have been "terminated" for some purposes and cannot participate in a number of tribal functions or partake of certain tribal benefits. Obviously, such an arrangement is not possible on most

---

98. The non-Indian population within the reservation boundaries is around 8,000. Tribal jurisdiction is not, of course, asserted over them.

other reservations, where the full-bloods constitute a far smaller percentage of the population and often are even in the minority, as, for example, among the Blackfeet, Sioux, and Chippewa, with less than 20 percent each. The aim of the Ute setup appears to be to prevent a development that has taken place on many of the reservations, in which the mixed-bloods often have come to occupy most of the positions of power to the exclusion of the full-bloods. (The Navajo tribe—like the Ute tribe, relatively unmixed— has no official policy or practice based on blood lines; one can nevertheless observe among the Navajo more subtle pressures and developments, some favoring full-bloods, others benefiting the mixed-bloods.)

It is especially difficult to get a grasp of the court situation on the Uintah and Ouray Reservation, which, with the exception of Fort Totten, has a lower volume of court business than the other reservations visited.[99] Also, although essentially as summary as elsewhere, the judicial process moves very slowly. The difference may be attributed in part to a smaller total population and lower density, but undoubtedly other subtle cultural factors are at play too. Also, the personality and behavior of the chief judge go far toward stamping the character of tribal court business; at the same time, of course, the judge himself reflects his reservation's atmosphere, customs, and institutions.

I was able to observe only "arraignments" in this court. The chief judge said that his practice was to hold trials once a month over a two-day period; when the time came for the trials to be held, however, he postponed them for another month, even though he had assured me in a telephone conversation on the workday immediately preceding the scheduled trial date that business would proceed as scheduled. The inability to observe full trials was unfortunate, because they are such rare events in the tribal courts generally. Here it was particularly so in view of the chief judge's assertion that trials in his tribal court were just like "regular" court proceedings, with a (white) prosecutor, (white) defense lawyers, and all. Anticipating a question about the nature of the tribal judge's role in these circumstances, he volunteers that he "runs" the court and keeps the professional lawyers "under control," an assertion that draws smiles from the police clerk and police officer who are taking part in the conversation. It is also contradicted by reports (from the tribal police and one of the white defense lawyers) that the young, inexperienced prosecutor is no match for the defense attorneys, which creates the usual tribal court imbalance problem. The chief judge's remarks are also made suspect by the observable fact

99. This assertion is supported by the observational evidence as well as by the court statistics I was able to collect. It is not supported by the AILIP figure given in note 46 *supra*. The reliability of that figure, however, is uncertain.

that he is not a very authoritative figure; neither the police nor the tribal council display much respect when dealing with him, and interviews with clerks, BIA officials, and jailed defendants lead to the same impression. The only local informant with anything positive to say about tribal justice was one of the white lawyers who handled cases in the tribal court from time to time. A beneficiary of the system (paying clients) and its imbalance (inexperienced prosecution), this lawyer felt that Uintah and Ouray justice was "pretty good," or "certainly no worse than the [white] J.P. system."[100]

The chief judge likes to orate at length in vague general terms about Indian justice, Indian traditions, and the distinctiveness of those traditions from white institutions and concepts. It is impossible to get him to be specific, however. Paradoxically, the Uintah and Ouray court process appears more geared to, and closer to achieving, what the chief judge derogatorily calls "anglo-ization" than, for example, the courts of Standing Rock or Fort Totten, where there was very little talk of Indian tradition. The chief judge's goals for the tribal court are also quite pedestrian when compared with his rhetoric about "Indianness." His number one objective is to get a new and separate building for the court; currently, the court is housed in the modest but adequate prefab law-and-order building shared with the police department. His greatest pride in "Indian" justice is in the fact that a divorce granted by him, in his court, can be upheld in places as far away as Los Angeles, as he reports happened one time. His "vision" for tribal justice is for his decisions to be upheld more often.

Total caseload statistics and a sample of the dispositional pattern of Uintah and Ouray tribal justice were presented earlier.[101] The dispositions showed a relatively harsh and moralistic system of criminalization, an assessment confirmed by Indians interviewed in the Fort Duchesne jail. The chief judge said that he varied his policies from time to time: "sometimes hard, sometimes lenient—it depends on what the people need." Other observers, notably one Uintah and Ouray Indian working for the BIA, saw tribal justice as being too lenient and having no impact. Interestingly enough, one finds such varied perceptions of court operations on each reservation visited. To some extent, this is explained by differences in perspectives and expectations, but it is also more than that. Generally and paradoxically, tribal justice can be both too harsh and too lenient. The real

---

100. The lawyers in the Salt Lake City firm that represents the tribe also speak favorably of the tribal court.

101. See pp. 32 and 50-51 *supra*. A funny but telling note on how quantitative information can be misunderstood (the tyranny of statistics?) came from the tribal official in charge of collecting such information. With reference to the high crime figures for 1974 (not available, incidentally), the official said, "That [1974] was bad year; we were glad when the new year came."

explanation is that it is too summary and arbitrary; it has too little relation to specific facts, and it is not based on coherent underlying policies, or any policies at all.

A description of cases (arraignments) observed in the Uintah and Ouray court will bear out the above assessment. Two explanatory notes about the Uintah and Ouray cases are in order: (1) all cases are handled by the chief judge even though the court has an associate judge (who was never in the court during any of the days of observations); (2) all cases involve adults, because juvenile matters are handled by a non-Indian state juvenile judge at Price, Utah, a town some 75 miles southwest of the political and popular center of the reservation.

Four arraignments are held one afternoon in the Uintah and Ouray court, which is called into session about 45 minutes after the scheduled time. The chief judge begins by "explaining" the trial rights in a long-winded fashion. Whether this is any more effective than the more common method of ritualistically reading off a constitutionally derived formula is debatable.

The first case involves the typical reservation charges of being drunk and disorderly and resisting arrest. The defendant, more aware and aggressive than the average Indian accused of these kinds of offenses, pleads not guilty. When the judge asks him if he will get a lawyer, the defendant says he will. A trial date is then set, and bond is set at $60 per charge for a total of $180. Bond seems rather high in view of the nature of the charges and the prevailing economic circumstances. Otherwise, however, the proceeding seems routine and well conducted.

The next few cases are more problematic, however. First comes an Indian man, about 30 years old, answering three complaints centering on nonsupport which have been lodged against him by his wife, who sits snickering in the spectator section. The defendant pleads not guilty, then confusion sets in. In setting the trial date, the chief judge realizes that there are several separable elements in the complaint and that they are separable along civil-criminal lines. Proceeding then to make such separations, he winds up setting two different trial dates. He also issues a restraining order, a favorite tribal court device, to keep the husband away from the wife, even though no evidence has been presented to justify this measure. At the end, no one seems quite certain about what has been decided or why.

This air of confusion is common in the tribal courts; the Uintah and Ouray court is not an exception. During the proceedings, the defendants sometimes fail to find out the most elementary aspect of their case, namely, what they are charged with. Dispositional determinations also remain a mystery to many participants. Since there is usually no bailiff or police present and since the judge maintains a posture of noncommunication, defendants hesitatingly wander back to their seats or out of the courtroom, trying to figure out whether, and if so where, they are to post bond, pay the fine, or be taken into custody for serving the jail sentence. Informality in court proceedings can be a good feature; but one doubts that this formless, directionless quality serves any sound purpose. It is particularly ironic to find such failure of communication in the tribal courts: one of the prime justifications for their existence must be that what goes on in them is, if nothing else, at least more comprehensible to Indians than what occurs in the outside courts.

At the same time, when informality might serve a purpose, it is—as in the domestic relations case above—abandoned in favor of needless formalism. Rather than handle the various grievances that grow out of one ongoing marital dispute in one proceeding, the court loses itself in an attempt to make spurious separations. No doubt inspired by the "Anglo" model, such differentiation of proceedings makes little sense in a tribal court in which no oppressive case volume exists, where the judges have no specialized legal skills or knowledge or supporting personnel who do, and where the same judge hears everything.

In the third case, a young Indian woman facing the usual drunk-and-disorderly type charge smirks a bit during the reading of the complaint, pleads guilty, and gets the choice between a $30 fine and a 20-day jail term. The judge gives her time—until the next paycheck—to come up with the money. There is no problem here.

The fourth case, another drunk-disorderly-type charge, is aggravated by the fact that the defendant's alleged behavior was in violation of one of these familiar restraining orders and by the further complaint that he fought the arresting police officer, who is not present. The defendant is one of these noncommunicative, broken human beings (similar to the skid-row types of the big cities) who are found in such abundance on the reservations—especially of course in the courthouse and jail. After initially mumbling something to the effect that he cannot remember, he ultimately pleads guilty to all charges. The judge accepts the plea and, because of the aggravating circumstances, sentences the man to 30 days in jail. This case illustrates two disturbing features of tribal justice: (1) it is so often at the arraignment stage—the so-called preliminary phase in which representation and deliberation are uniformly absent—that crucial dispositive decisions are made; and (2) these dispositions can be quite harsh.

INDIAN TRIBES
UNDER STATE AND COUNTY JURISDICTION

Whatever the problems of tribal court operations, one justification offered for their creation and continued operation is that the Indians would fare far worse in white courts. To test this allegation, I visited several reservations (tribes) operating under state and county jurisdiction and also took a look at county and district court operations in areas immediately adjacent to reservations with tribal courts. It was not possible, of course, within the limits of this study, to do a full investigation of the integrated experience.

The North Carolina Cherokees

The Eastern Cherokees in North Carolina are a remnant of one of the dominant Indian tribes of the American colonial period. The Cherokee tribe once inhabited an area that covered much of present-day Georgia and portions of what are now South Carolina, North Carolina, Alabama, and Tennessee, until most of its population was moved to the Oklahoma territories[102] in the 1830s. The Eastern Cherokees—numbering between 5,000 and 6,000 today—are thus among the Indians who have had most prolonged contact with white society. Despite this, many of them still maintain an existence in the mountains of North Carolina which is to some extent distinct and separate from that of the whites in the area. (There are formal reservation boundaries, and being "Indian" entitles one to certain unique federal benefits and liabilities.) This separation is probably maintained both for sociocultural and for commercial reasons. The Cherokees' awareness of their Indian identity has been a persistent phenomenon despite the powerful forces of acculturation and assimilation. It is also a fact that there are not many recognizable Indians left in the eastern states, and tourism in the Smoky Mountains is not hurt by the eagerness of many white families to come to see "real Indians." Not surprisingly, therefore, the town of Cherokee (the main one on the reservation) is saturated with curio shops and motels in the shape of, or guarded by, outsized wooden or plastic tepees, buffaloes, bears, and braves. During the summer months, many of the Cherokees find employment in the tourist business. (A fair number of tourist concerns are actually owned and operated by Indians, which is far more rare on the western reservations.) Some spend their time "chiefing," which means standing in front of one of the curio shops dressed up in the kind of combination east-west-plainsman-woodsman-hunter-warrior outfit that only the most geographically and culturally schizophrenic Indian could even imagine wearing, but they resemble the Hollywood Indian closely enough to attract the undiscriminating tourist. By the time anyone gets close enough to detect the "chief's" levis and

---

102. See Thurman Wilkins, Cherokee Tragedy: The Story of the Ridge Family and the Decimation of a People (New York: Macmillan Co., 1970), and Rennard Strickland, Fire and the Spirits: Cherokee Law from Clan to Court (Norman: University of Oklahoma Press, 1975).

unpolished black shoes protruding from underneath the conglomeration of leather and feathers, the mission has been accomplished.

While they are thus Indians for some purposes, and by not-too-strict racial or ethnic standards,[103] the Cherokees do not have their own tribal court. They resort instead to the state and county court system, primarily that of Swain County (Bryson City) and Jackson County (Sylva); and for some matters, to the federal courts. There is something akin to a "tribal" police force; that is, a number of Cherokees have been deputized by the counties to handle most of the on-reservation law-enforcement problems, while white officers on the sheriff's force concentrate mainly on off-reservation matters and individuals.

Cherokee attitudes toward their treatment in the white court system are fairly favorable. One may hear some general complaints about discrimination or nonresponsiveness, but these perceptions are seldom supported by concrete instances, let alone verifiable facts. Not only are complaints of this order vague, but most of them are accompanied by the qualification that this is the way things were in the past and that today the situation is better. Also, most of the complaints about nonresponsiveness appear to be traceable primarily to the fact that the Cherokee Reservation is located in two counties bordering on a national park (with small tracts in several additional counties), which results in much confusion over jurisdiction in the areas of major crimes, conservation issues, and tribal concerns as well as individual problems. In a few circles, there is talk about the Cherokees' establishing a tribal court of their own, but it is primarily based on metaphysical notions of Cherokee sovereignty rather than on concrete disenchantment with the current state and county setup.[104]

Direct observation of the court processes affecting the Cherokees tends to confirm that there are few grounds for major complaints. Surely there are minor shortcomings, but they appear to affect whites as well as Cherokees, and they are not systematically at odds with what can be expected of the administration of justice in the real world.

A magistrate's, or justice of the peace (J.P.), system is operative in the counties in which the Cherokee Reservation is located. These magistrates, who are white, are comparable with tribal court judges in terms of their lack of formal legal training and their lack of prestige and status, but they have far less jurisdiction. In very minor matters, they accept guilty pleas

---

103. In fact, there does not seem to be much more intermixture with whites on the Cherokee Reservation than on many western, let alone midwestern, reservations—where it is very substantial; there are still full-blood and near full-blood Cherokees.

104. The tribal administration has recently jumped on the separatism bandwagon and has asked one of its (white) tribal attorneys to look into the possibility of retrocession.

and make settlements. But both in theory and in practice, one may take matters to a higher court (to the county or district court) more easily than one can in the reservation tribal courts, in which there is rarely a genuine contest and even more rarely an appeal. Here, once a matter is actually in the county or district court, with professional judges, lawyers, and sometimes the press and other interested observers, professionals, or bystanders present, the proceedings become radically different from those that are typical in the tribal courts. The procedure is open and has an adversary nature, unlike the essentially closed and one-sided workings of the tribal courts.[105]

The following descriptions of county court proceedings that involved Cherokees will illustrate these points. The cases are from the Jackson County court, housed in a historic but modernized building overlooking the idyllic town of Sylva. (Jackson County appears to be prosperous; Swain County and its county seat, Bryson City, are by comparison more depressed. But in the 1960s and early 1970s, the whole North Carolina mountain area experienced a tremendous economic upswing from the poverty and isolation that prevailed before that time.) In the court, about half or slightly more than half of the parties and spectators are Cherokees, as are all the defendants in the cases described. Court and law-enforcement officials acknowledge that the percentage of Indian criminal defendants is disproportionately high in relation to their representation in the total population of Jackson County.

In the first case, a Cherokee woman in her late twenties or early thirties, has been charged with driving while under the influence of alcohol. She is represented by a young lawyer who recently graduated from the University of Tennessee Law School and who holds a job that is somewhat analogous to public defender for the Cherokee Reservation.[106] The Cherokees often hire local private lawyers to represent them in civil as well as criminal cases; when they are financially unable to do so in criminal cases, the county court appoints a lawyer for them from a rotating list of the local private bar. The name of this particular "public defender" is one of those listed; and in criminal cases in the *federal* court, it is always he who is appointed to represent indigent Cherokee defendants.

One of the assistant prosecutors from the district attorney's office,

---

105. Of course, the Anglo-American system, even operating at its best, is bound by its own rituals of adversary contest and other substantive and procedural peculiarities. The point is not to endorse the Anglo system per se, but to point out that compared with poor imitations of it, namely, the tribal court operations, it looks quite good.

106. The lawyer, to be precise, is employed by the Eastern Cherokee Legal Services Organization, a private foundation.

which serves several counties, is handling the case for the county. He calls
four police officers—all mixed-blood Cherokees—who were involved in the
arrest and booking. All give more or less the same testimony about seeing
the defendant's car weaving on the road, smelling liquor on her breath,
watching her stagger out of the car and at the station house. The defense
does not have much to go on in response to this. A fairly weak cross-
examination of the police officers is conducted. Perhaps the smell of alcohol was on her *clothes* rather than on her breath? They only *saw* her
stagger—that is only fallible observation? And so forth. It becomes clear
that the only strategy with any potential for success is for the defense to
plead for leniency, which is done by citing personal difficulties that have
recently befallen the defendant. The judge, however, is apparently not
impressed and sentences her to one year in the women's reformatory.

At first glance, this result appears quite harsh. But later, in private, the
public defender says that the judge really had little choice; the record
before the court showed that this was the defendant's fifth arrest for
drunken driving in the past few years. Also, she is known (less officially) to
be one of the biggest bootleggers and drug-pushers on the reservation. The
defender adds that he will exercise the automatic right to appeal from the
county court to the superior court; he believes he may be able to get the
sentence reduced ("bargained down") in the higher court, where the predis-
position toward individualized justice is less strong and where there may be
concessions in return for his not fully contesting the case.

The defender adds some gratuitous assessments about prosecution and
court personnel in the area: the prosecutors are quite reasonable and non-
vindictive; they are local men, who know and understand the people—
Indians and whites—and the situations of the area; also, they are generally
quite cooperative toward the defense. The judges are given a similar assessment: they, too, are reasonable; a couple of them periodically like to give
young defense attorneys a hard time, but it is mostly bark and very little
bite. The judges are local men as well; they know the Cherokees; they hunt
and fish with them in their spare time.

The defendant in the next case is a Cherokee man in his early twenties.
He has a local private attorney (who later states that a good number of the
Cherokees can afford counsel's fees in these types of cases: "Hell, many of
them pay better [more dependably] than the whites"). The charges are
driving while under the influence of alcohol and reckless driving. The
prosecution elicits the usual testimony from the arresting police officers
about seeing the defendant driving in an erratic manner, and so forth. The
twist to this case is that the police gave, or tried to give, the defendant a
breath test in the Jackson County station house in Sylva (this option was
not available in the previous case, where the arrest and booking took place
in the town of Cherokee on the reservation). In addition, a half-empty
six-pack of beer was found in the defendant's car.

The breath-testing device, when used on the defendant, registered nothing. The police insist this is because the defendant blew out of the side of his mouth each time he was tested (four times). The defense, of course, argues that the defendant simply was not drunk or that the machine was not working. Nothing conclusive is developed by either side, and the breath test issue remains up in the air. The defense goes on to present testimony by the defendant himself, who reports that he drank only one of the three beers, the other two having been drunk by friends he went to pick up. The prosecution counters by extracting from the defendant the admission that he was thoroughly drunk the night preceding the arrest, a circumstance implying that one beer would have been enough to (re)incapacitate him.

The judge's verdict, though not inconsistent with the facts as developed during the trial, is in essence a compromise: not guilty on the charge of driving while intoxicated and guilty on the charge of reckless driving. The disposition is a $50 fine, which upon his counsel's request the defendant is given one week (until the next court date) to pay. Everyone seems satisfied with this result; the Cherokee defendant and his lawyer chat about the case afterward, indicating a good general rapport as well as satisfaction with the specific outcome.

The Oklahoma Tribes

In Oklahoma, I made visits to areas populated by the Creek, Osage, Pawnee, and Western Cherokee tribes. The Pawnee and Osage are plains tribes; the Cherokee and Creek tribes were transplanted to the Oklahoma Territory from the East[107] in the first half of the nineteenth century, and thus are further away from their roots, both geographically and culturally, than are the Plains Indians. Although there are no "reservations" proper in Oklahoma,[108] the Indians often live lives that are to some degree segregated. The extent of separation varies from tribe to tribe and from area to area. The Creek, Cherokee, and Osage people live in relatively well-integrated surroundings; towns like Okmulgee, Tahlequah, and Pawhuska—the county seats—are populated by Indians, whites, and mixed-bloods. Yet these Indians have not altogether abandoned tribal trappings: they still have tribal councils (now more ceremonial than anything else), and the ubiquitous BIA still plays a limited role, operating out of agency offices of sorts. On the negative side, it appeared that people of unequivocal Indian

---

107. The Cherokee and Creek are two of what are known as the "Five Civilized Tribes"; the others are the Chickasaw, Choctaw, and Seminole.

108. The Osage area in Oklahoma has occasionally been identified as a "reservation." The explanation may lie in the fact that the mineral holdings of the area are "tribally" owned. By some interpretations this apparently suffices to give the land in question reservation status.

ancestry were underrepresented (though not unrepresented) in important political, professional, and management jobs. No doubt the reasons for this situation are more complex and vexing than those implied in the simple charge of "discrimination." The Pawnee situation, with a substantial degree of separation from non-Indian society, was reported to be similar to that of the less "acculturated" (Plains) tribes in western Oklahoma. Pawnee people were to be seen in all parts of the county seat of Pawnee, and they occupied some municipal posts, but they, like the blacks, lived in a separate section of the town. Historical factors have played an important part in producing this living pattern: land allotments were originally made on an Indian/non-Indian basis, and subsequently the federal government (through BIA and HUD) has had a hand in perpetuating the pattern by building Indian housing and service centers (e.g., the "Indian hospital") on the allotted lands. Other, more subtle social factors no doubt figure, too, in producing the segregation.

With the above in mind, it is not surprising that some complaints surface about the discriminatory treatment of Indians by white officials. As in North Carolina, however, those Indians who voice such complaints do not see the problems as serious or systematic; white officials, of course, unanimously and vigorously deny all. Observations and interviews failed to turn up evidence of a deleterious situation. Court cases involving Indians appeared to be handled in the same way as those involving whites. Occasionally, the speech of certain law-enforcement officials betrayed mild forms of paternalism toward some Indian people or annoyance with certain Indian individuals ("a few troublemakers") or habits (annual pow-wow that "disrupted" town life). Often, however, Indians themselves exhibited the same reactions to the same individuals or practices.

In Pawnee, I observed an arraignment involving two mixed-blood juveniles charged with possession of marijuana. At this stage of the case, the defendants are without counsel, but their parents are present. A conference with the prosecutor has already taken place, at which all parties have agreed to a disposition of probation without conviction (so that no juvenile criminal record is created). The proceedings before the judge—in chambers rather than in the courtroom—are held merely to formalize the agreement. The judge takes the time to explain the conditions of probation and asks questions of both parents and juveniles to see if they have understood the terms of and the alternatives to this probation "agreement." It is difficult to find fault with this deliberate process, which preserves the sense of privacy provided by law in juvenile matters.

After the proceedings, in private conversation, the judge (white) reveals himself to be one who believes strongly in the kind of individualized and usually lenient justice that seeks to exhaust local resources in dealing with problems before turning—in "hopeless" cases—to those of the state. The case just observed was certainly in tune with that. When questioned about possible discrimination, he launches into a bit of a sermon about how whites and Indians are treated equally in his court and, as far as he knows, in the town of Pawnee generally. As a local man who has practiced law and been a judge in the area his whole adult life, he knows all the people, their backgrounds, and current circumstances. (The judge, incidentally, is literally blind. It does not necessarily follow that race could therefore not influence him, because to one so familiar with the community a litigant's name would be a giveaway.) Asked about the matter of guilty pleas, the judge responds that he frequently refuses them from both Indians and whites when he is convinced that they do not understand the alternatives and ramifications.

Pawhuska, county seat of Osage County (and Osage country), is a relatively prosperous town. Early in the twentieth century, oil was discovered on Indian-held lands, and many Osages became wealthy by selling the land or by leasing drilling rights to it. An influx of professionals—businessmen, lawyers, etc.—accompanied the industrial development of the area. Intermarriage among Indians and whites became frequent. Now the diminishing income from the oil fields is so spread out among the many heirs of Osage descent that it no longer suffices to fully support many of them. But other holdovers from the earlier period remain intact. Race relations are apparently not a problem; too many people have some Indian blood. Indians or mixed-bloods are well represented in local government and in law-enforcement positions. Until recently, the associate district judge was an Osage.

In the Osage County court I observed a preliminary hearing for an attempted murder. The case involved two black families who had been acquainted for generations and who lived virtually on top of each other on the outskirts of Pawhuska. The proceedings were so thorough and detailed that I was surprised to learn at the end that this was only the preliminary hearing. The defendant, a man in his thirties, is represented by a very colorful private attorney, who was seen earlier that day conducting some business at the Pawnee courthouse. The state's main witnesses are a man and his two high-school-age sons. One boy, the victim, had been shot in the hand. The defense attorney, who is white (as are the prosecutor and judge), lays into the prosecution witnesses, suggesting possible motives and circumstances that could have led to misidentification of the attacker. But the witnesses handle it well; they are not intimidated, and they stick to a consistent version of what took place. The defense attorney treats the white arresting officer in the same—sometimes almost insulting, occasionally humorous—fashion. What the line of the defense might be at trial does not become clear, but the defendant pleads not guilty.

Both the prosecution and the defense are thorough and give an impression of competence, or at least of dedication to the case. Noteworthy, and apparent throughout the hearing, is the fact that this is a very personal affair; all those involved in the proceedings know each other. Despite this fact and the fact that all the disputants are black and all the professionals are white, there appears to be a healthy adversary tone to the proceedings.

Afterward, conversations with the officials reveal that elements of paternalism and condescension are not lacking in the attitudes of local whites toward blacks and Indians. Some resentment is expressed, especially with reference to the Indians, about how the "minorities" get so much help from the government these days that it is the average white who has become disadvantaged. To these whites, the notion that the Indian is down-trodden and neglected has become a gigantic and ironic hoax. In rural Oklahoma, blacks constitute a more genuinely underprivileged class than do the Indians. Indeed, if poverty, dependency, and perceptions of discrimination justify separate and autonomous juridical status—as sometimes, perversely enough, appears to be the case made for the Indian tribal courts—then rural blacks in Oklahoma have a pretty good argument.[109]

In Tahlequah, Cherokee Indian country, nothing can be observed that seriously shakes confidence in the capacity of the state court system to deal with the Indian population. As usual, there are some faint rumblings of dissatisfaction, but nothing serious or concrete is cited. For example, the half-Cherokee BIA superintendent in Tahlequah mentions the findings of a study done for the governor's commission, headed by a part-Creek lawyer, to the effect that in Oklahoma Indians have a higher arrest rate than whites. What inferences may be drawn from these findings are not clear; it is likely that the Indians have a higher alcoholism rate than whites, too, a fact which is equally difficult to interpret but which may help explain some of the arrest disparity.

Two arraignments are held in the Tahlequah court. The accused in the first case has been charged with driving while intoxicated and is ready to plead guilty. The judge, however, extracts from him the information that he has been in touch with a lawyer about the case and urges him to follow up on this. The upshot is that the accused's father goes out and returns a few minutes later with the lawyer. After a 15-minute conference outside the courtroom, the defendant and lawyer return to plead not guilty. Bond is set and time is given for the defendant to come up with the cash.

The second case is more problematic. It involves a young Cherokee man charged with failure to pay the $25 fine that resulted from an earlier charge of "disturbing the peace," to which he had pleaded guilty, and with

---

109. It may be noted that in few places does racial prejudice against blacks remain as strong as it does on the Indian reservations. In North Carolina, one of the lawyers involved in representing the Cherokees said that he could not hire a black student assistant, as he had wished, because the Cherokees would not accept this. The Five Civilized Tribes, both in the East and in Oklahoma, even have a black slaveholding past in common with the whites.

failure to answer a bench warrant issued subsequently. The young man, who has no lawyer, explains that he has been in jail in another county on a marijuana charge. In view of the fact that the accused has just finished a jail term, the judge sees no point in further punishment and suspends the original fine and related charges. A stern lecture follows—with what effect, one cannot tell. The accused appears to be one of these noncommunicative, lost souls, without lawyer or relative to help him out, of whom one sees so many in the tribal courts. In the Oklahoma areas I visited, this appeared to be an isolated case.

Okmulgee, Oklahoma, is in Creek territory, but Seminoles and Cherokees also live in the area. The Indians in Okmulgee are in a better position than the blacks, who live apart in a relatively large, very depressed-looking section. Indians are reported to be well represented in county and municipal government and in other key positions. The chief of police is half-Creek; two attorneys practicing out of offices on the court-house square are part Creek.

Interviews with the local magistrate and judge yield an important point about the handling of guilty pleas in Okmulgee. Their story is that accused—both white and Indian—often come in at arraignment with the intention to plead guilty, but both judges say that they frequently resist these attempts on grounds that the decisions are not fully understood and considered. The court then appoints attorneys to help in the deliberation on the best strategy for the accused.

A case observed in the Okmulgee court appears to confirm the judge's statements. A 16-year-old white boy is charged with delinquency after being caught sniffing glue at some gathering of young folks. The boy is noncommunicative and hostile—primarily toward his parents, who are present—and just wants to cut short the proceedings by pleading guilty. The judge does not let him do so; he appoints an attorney and says he will accept a plea only after the attorney has been consulted. After the case, the judge indicates privately that he thinks the juvenile has a good chance of getting off on evidentiary grounds with the help of an attorney. What worries him, though, is his impression that the parents have no control over the boy and that he may not see the attorney or show up for the next hearing. The judge considered setting bond rather than releasing the boy in his parents' "custody" but decided against it because the burden of coming up with the money would have fallen on the parents, who are poor, and because the prosecution did not press for it.

On the whole, the system in Oklahoma appears to work well. Time is taken to consider cases from various legal and personal angles. Professional services are used (and are provided at no cost to those who cannot pay for them) to present these angles with what seems to be a fair measure of expertise and competence. The justice process in rural Oklahoma seems preferable to the one-sidedness and the lack of inquiry that so often characterize tribal court operations, as well as to the rush and impersonality of urban proceedings.

The Minnesota Tribes

Observations of the court procedures and interviews with court personnel on the Minnesota reservations will be treated only briefly and generally here so as not to belabor points already made.

The chairman of the Red Lake Band of Chippewa denied me access to the Red Lake Reservation tribal court—the only major one in Minnesota[110]—for a variety of reasons; for example, the Indian people had already been studied to death, and little good had come of it;[111] and whites should not be telling Indians what to do anyway. Beneath the surface, however, there were more defensive motives as well: at the time, a great election dispute was taking place, in which the tribal chairman and the court judges were central figures; the reputation of and the public confidence in the Red Lake tribal court was at a low point (according to Indian informants from the Red Lake and Leech Lake reservations); and only a few years earlier the Red Lake system of justice had been the subject of a very uncomplimentary article in the *North Dakota Law Review*.[112]

The focus is thus on the Leech Lake and White Earth reservations, the major reservations that are under state and county jurisdiction in Minnesota.

White Earth and Leech Lake reservations are checkerboard areas of Indian and white landholdings, matched by an alternating pattern of small towns and villages that are predominantly Indian or predominantly white. Some of the area within the reservation "boundaries" is state forest property. Tourism is a primary industry; many, mostly modest, "resorts" and individual summer homes and cabins surround the lakes that dot the region. Most of the resorts are owned and operated by whites, but occasionally one finds places run by individuals who are at least part Chippewa.

These living and working patterns indicate that, notwithstanding the juridical integration, full social and economic integration of these Minnesota Indians has not been achieved. In fact, one has the impression that a greater separation exists between the Indians and the whites in northern

---

110. In 1972, a tiny reservation in the northeastern corner of Minnesota, Nett Lake (Bois Forte) Reservation, also assumed tribal jurisdiction.

111. One cannot help but sympathize with this point of view. The chairman added the question: "What if I came to Chicago and said I wanted to study you?"

112. Note, Tribal Injustice: The Red Lake Court of Indian Offenses, 48 N.D.L. Rev. 639 (1972).

Minnesota than in eastern Oklahoma. There is also a perceptible movement among the Minnesota Indians to maintain and even reinforce this separation, although support for this movement is hardly unanimous among the Indians, let alone the local whites. Curiously enough, the loudest, most determined talk about Indian separatism—in Minnesota and elsewhere—seems to come from "Indians" with a substantial percentage of white blood and from "outsider" whites from Minneapolis, Chicago, or other large cities. Presumably, the mixedbloods, who have often attained leadership or spokesman positions on the reservation, have most to gain from maintaining Indian separatism. Outsider whites, of course, have nothing to lose in supporting the romantic ideal of Indian separatism: the price for maintaining or returning to such separation in the 1970s does not fall on them.

On the White Earth Reservation, one of the most interesting and valuable informants was a mixed-blood owner and operator of a large resort. Not surprisingly, since he was also former deputy sheriff, the man presented a rather uncompromising law-and-order point of view. When first encountered, he and a white deputy sheriff were holding a meeting with some 20-30 young "Indian" (almost all mixed-blood) men and women on the subject of the alleged law-enforcement discrimination against Indians on that part of the reservation. On the reservation, as in many parts of white society, young people, for lack of anything more productive to do, often wind up spending their evenings hot-rodding or simply cruising through town looking for something nonproductive to do—sometimes after drinking. The particular problem in White Earth is that many of the young people like to emphasize their part-Indian heritage by letting their hair grow long and that the resort business located just outside the town depends on white tourism. The individuals who run the resorts, even if they are of Indian heritage themselves, are likely to be overprotective of what they presume to be the sensitivities of white tourists and hence are very unsympathetic to wild-looking young "Indians" driving or hanging around. They are quick to call in the police and sometimes try to take "the law" into their own hands. The upshot is an unhealthy climate, with the resort owners and the "kids" as opponents and the police caught in the middle.

It is probably a sign of progress that the meeting referred to took place at all. Nothing conclusive was agreed upon; nothing very concrete transpired; but at least grievances were aired and some pent-up bitterness was released. The mixed-blood ex-deputy began with what was essentially a defensive monologue, but after a while the young people interrupted with contradictions and accusations. The white deputy just listened. Gradually some sort of mutual understanding, if no specific agreement, emerged, and the number of smiles and jokes interspersing the "debate" increased. Then the meeting broke up.

Later, in private, the resort owner volunteered that what he perceived as a senseless revival of separatist notions contributed heavily to the problems on the White Earth Reservation. Because of it, he said, Indians expected favors or advantages based on racial distinctions that in many cases were hardly detectable. In his view (that of a mixed-blood who has "made" it), the state and county court and law-enforcement system on White Earth worked well enough; the suggestion of tribal courts was laughable. He backed up his reaction by pointing to the complete breakdown of the White Earth tribe's attempts to run its own political affairs; the third council election in the past half year was just coming up, the previous two having been invalidated on grounds of fraud.[113] Corruption in the White Earth tribal government was rampant, he said, and he (like several other informants) singled out the chairman as one of the major culprits. Finally, he added, from what he knew of them, the tribal government and court on Red Lake Reservation were perfect examples of the fact that the Indians in Minnesota were incapable of running their own affairs.

Similar points of view were expressed by several other White Earth Reservation people. One Indian couple who worked with juveniles expressed the view that the Indians could not run their own court "at this stage." Corruption, waste, and the total ineffectiveness of the current tribal government were cited in support of their conviction. The couple, however, also expressed reservations about the state and county system of justice: "They play favorites too—you can never win against a cop or against the sheriff or his deputies."

Another informant who took a jaundiced view of tribal courts was a captain on the town police force—a full-blood Chippewa. In his opinion, the state and county system worked well when, as here, Indians occupied some important posts in the system. As police captain, he had received good support from the white community and white officialdom, even when he became involved at one point in his career in the arrest and charging of the son of the (white) chief of police. Most of the trouble he had had, he said, was from some persons, including the White Earth Tribal chairman, within the Indian community and from Indian or Indian-sympathizer outsider groups. This was "politics," in his opinion, and one of the major reasons why Indian self-government could not work.

Often, as above, the information given by Indians who have done well in an integrated setting tends to be self-serving. However, it is not thereby necessarily unpersuasive, nor does it run counter to the indications of experience or observation.

---

113. For some of the formal history and resolution of the dispute, see Indian Political Action Comm. v. Tribal Executive Comm., 416 F. Supp. 655 (D. Minn. 1976). For similar problems on the Red Lake Reservation, see White v. Tribal Council, 383 F. Supp. 810 (D. Minn. 1974).

On Leech Lake Reservation, a familiar pattern of views could be discerned. The white Legal Services attorneys who were working for the tribe out of an office in Cass Lake and who were exploring the legal and political steps relevant to the consideration of "restoration" of tribal jurisdiction on Leech Lake Reservation, did most of the talking about Indian self-determination and sovereignty. Words like "nationhood" were bandied about as rationalizations for this drive toward restoration. The attorneys conceded that the state and county court systems were operating satisfactorily with respect to Indians and recognized a white private attorney from a nearby town as one of the staunchest defenders of Indian clients in the state court. In the next breath, however, the OEO people lapsed into slogans about Indian sovereignty, or they rehashed old tales about Indians' being refused drinks in off-reservation bars or about the white police having coerced sober and law-abiding Indians during snowstorms into shoveling snow around the police station, jail, or courthouse.

A similar line was taken by one of the rising young politicians on the Leech Lake Reservation, a college dropout and three-quarters white (qualifications that seem to go a long way on some reservations). To hear him talk about restoration, sovereignty, and "getting out from under 280,"[114] one would think that he was setting policy for tribes in pre-Columbian times instead of for a small band of mostly mixed-bloods, surrounded and already almost absorbed by white society.

More realistic points of view were expressed. One middle-aged informant (full-blood or close to it) who hung around the tribal offices stated emphatically that installing a tribal court on Leech Lake Reservation would be "a big mess"; one only had to look at the operations of the Leech Lake tribal government to come to this conclusion. Also, the current brief experience with a tribal conservation court (jurisdiction over fish and game violations on the reservation) augured ill; from its inception, the operations of that court had been marred by political problems, and the Indian conservation judge had just quit under pressure. In the informant's opinion, there was little reason to be more sanguine about the establishment of a standard tribal court. Finally, to back up his view, he recounted his experience of getting "picked up" on the Red Lake Reservation, about 40 miles to the north, and taken before the tribal court there: "I got all-too-quick justice—a real kangaroo court."

Similar opinions were voiced by the public defender in one of the neighboring towns, a young white lawyer with two years of experience with Legal Services on Leech Lake Reservation and familiar with tribal

---

114. The reference is to Public Law 280, the termination legislation of 1953. See note 6 *supra*.

operations. From what he had seen take place in the Red Lake tribal court, the institution was without a shred of legitimacy: "90 percent of the cases could be successfully appealed [in theory] because of gross errors committed by the trial court." The only thing that saved the tribal court, he felt (wrongly one is inclined to say), was that it was a court of limited jurisdiction; therefore "gross injustices" occurred in only relatively minor cases with relatively minor consequences. Extending tribal court jurisdiction to serious cases (major crimes)—a frequent proposal these days—would change that situation and would in his estimation be "intolerable."

STATE COURTS NEAR RESERVATIONS

To collect additional comparative information, observations were made and interviews were conducted in state and county courts in areas bordering reservations with tribal courts: Gallup, Farmington, and Aztec, New Mexico—all just outside the Navajo Reservation; McIntosh, South Dakota, outside the Standing Rock Sioux Reservation; Devils Lake, North Dakota, outside the Fort Totten Reservation; and Roosevelt, Utah, just outside the Uintah and Ouray Ute Indian Reservation. Most of the observed cases involved whites, and most of the court and law-enforcement personnel were white. To describe all in detail seems excessive. In general, the system in these rural areas seemed to work well enough, and in most instances, the officials seemed to be reasonably conscientious, fair, and effective. One proceeding will be discussed in detail to illustrate the general experience and to make a specific comparison between the tribal court system and the outside justice of the peace (J.P.) system.

In Roosevelt, Utah, a predominantly white town only seven miles from Fort Duchesne, the Uintah and Ouray "capital," the J.P. system is still operative.[115] How it works is important in view of a frequent last-ditch defense of the tribal court system: "at least it's no worse, and maybe even better, than the J.P. system."

The Roosevelt J.P.'s "office" is a slightly set-off desk in a converted garage that now functions as an office-supply store. There is nothing pretentious about the place—just yards of pencils, pens, erasers, and stationery everywhere. The J.P., a very folksy and down-to-earth middle-aged man, was once in the banking business and much more affluent. On this particular morning, there is an assault and battery case, just a fight really, up for arraignment. The complaining witness shows up first, and the J.P. talks to him in such a way—jabbing him playfully with a penknife at one point—that by the time the accused arrives the notion of going any further with the case is abandoned. The two young men leave the office (store) more as friends than as adversaries.

---

115. For other references to the J.P. system, see pp. 127-31 *supra*, on North Carolina.

It is good for the J.P. to get the above case out of the way, because a more significant, more time-consuming matter is coming up, that of a 20-year-old white charged with driving while intoxicated. It turns out this will be a full-fledged trial, with attorneys on both sides. It will have to be held in the Roosevelt municipal building; the makeshift J.P.'s office will not do for this proceeding. First, a jury must be assembled. This is accomplished by the J.P.'s getting two impromptu helpers—boys known to him—to collect eight "disinterested parties" (people who know nothing about the case) off the Roosevelt streets (or out of the stores and offices). It is possible that the boys have some directions or a jury list to work with in collecting the jurors, but the impression is that they do not. In about 45 minutes, eight people have been rounded up—a mix of men and women, young and old. One is a gas-station attendant, two are white-collar types, and the rest of indeterminate occupations. There are no Indians in the group; few Indians appear to *live* in Roosevelt, but one does see many (especially older men) sitting around on street benches and in the stores and bars. One wonders whether an effort would have been made to collect some of the Indian transients (or residents) as jurors if the defendant had been Indian.[116]

Before the trial begins, the prosecutor and defense attorney each get a chance to make two challenges to the composition of the jury. They exercise this fully, with the result that the final jury consists of only two men and two women. While the jury collecting and selecting is taking place, I have time for an informal interview with a Utah state trooper, one of the complaining witnesses. He utters the by-now-familiar opinion about tribal courts, namely, that they are a "joke." (Identical phraseology was used by several other informants from widely separated parts of the country.) The trooper's main complaint is that the tribal court he knows about, the Ute tribal court, is "too lenient" and "too political." As to the politics, he cites several cases, in which he himself played the part of arresting officer and complaining witness, which involved tribal council leaders and relatives charged with driving while intoxicated. The court let them all off, he says, but "at least we made them [the council members] lose face, which is a big thing on the reservation." Apart from their courts, the trooper claims to like the Utes. As noted before, others charge that the tribal court is often too harsh, and both documents (the dispositions) and observations exist to that effect. The correct assessment is probably that the tribal court is too arbitrary. It may also be that police officers are always unhappy about the performance (especially the perceived leniency) of courts.

---

116. During the time of my visit in Gallup, New Mexico, 20 miles from the Navajo Reservation, the grand jury included at least three (possibly four) Indians (judging by sight).

The primary prosecution witnesses are the trooper and a fellow officer who arrested the defendant. The case against the defendant is impaired by the fact that the breath-testing machine, the tests of which the defendant was willing to undergo, was "inoperable" at the crucial time. All the prosecution is left with are one trooper's observations on the road and both troopers' account of certain simple-minded physical coordination tests conducted at the station house. In addition, the following facts emerge: because the breath-testing gadgetry was not working, one of the troopers took the accused to the hospital for a blood test, where the latter "got scared of the needle" and refused to take the test. Upon returning from the hospital to the station house, the trooper admittedly told the defendant, "Now your attorney won't have anything to work with to get you off," whereupon the defendant said he was willing to go back to the hospital to take the blood test after all. The trooper then refused, saying that the defendant "had had his chance."

The facts were fully developed by the attorneys on both sides. One of the troopers was required by the defense lawyer to do a demonstration of the physical coordination test given to the defendant, which consisted of routine exercises such as touching the nose while balancing on one leg with the eyes closed. The trooper lost his balance a number of times before successfully finding his nose. Other circumstances were brought under consideration: the defendant was tired the night of his arrest; he testified that he had been up since six o'clock that morning, had milked the cows, and had done other farm chores. The J.P. meanwhile was in complete control and handled the proceedings adroitly: his earlier informality and playfulness was replaced by a firmness and decisiveness in handling the attorneys, ruling on their infrequent objections, and generally keeping the proceedings on course.

After the lawyers had made extravagant closing arguments, the jury deliberated for 20 minutes and returned a verdict of not guilty—the only one possible on the facts. One wondered at that point what the troopers thought about the J.P. court. Actually, they did not seem resentful or crestfallen; they took the result in stride.